From Zero to Design Hero

The Ultimate Beginner's Guide

Contents

Chapters

1.What Is Graphic Design?

• An introduction to graphic design and why it matters.

• Real-world examples: logos, packaging, posters, and more.

• Inspirational case study: the Nike logo.

• Practical exercise: Analyze your favorite logo.

2.Tools of the Trade

• What you need to get started: iPad, Procreate, Canva, and other tools.

• A comparison of software options for beginners.

• Practical tips for setting up your workspace.

• Exercise: Get comfortable with your tools by creating a simple design.

3.Building Blocks: Shapes, Lines, and Textures

• How to use basic elements like shapes and lines in design.

• Adding texture for depth and interest.

• Practical exercise: Create a balanced composition using only circles and lines.

4.Working with Clients: From Brief to Design

• What to Do When Working with Clients

• How to Get the Right Brief

• The Process of Working with Clients

• Finalizing the Design

• The Psychology of Client Work

5.The Power of Color

• How colors influence emotions and decisions.

• Real-life examples: McDonald's, Tiffany & Co., and other brands.

• Practical exercise: Create a color palette for an imaginary brand.

6.Fonts and Typography

• Choosing and pairing fonts effectively.

• Tips to avoid common typography mistakes.

• Practical exercise: Design a poster using two contrasting fonts.

7.How to Create Your First Logo

• What makes a logo effective.

• Step-by-step guide to creating a logo.

• Real-life case studies: Nike and Airbnb.

• Practical exercise: Design a logo for a fictional coffee shop.

8.Patterns and Textures

• How to create repeating patterns and use textures.

• Tips for using patterns in branding or packaging.

• Practical exercise: Design a simple pattern for a product package.

9.Designing for Social Media

• Key principles for social media graphics: format, colors, and typography.

• Examples of effective designs on Instagram and TikTok.

• Practical exercise: Create a post for Instagram using simple elements.

10.Finding Your Creative Voice

• How to discover your unique style as a designer.

• Inspiration from real designers and design communities.

• Practical exercise: Create a design that reflects your personality.

11.Creating a Brand Identity

• What is Brand Identity?

• Key Elements of Brand Identity

- How to Create a Brand Identity

- How to Maintain Consistency in Your Brand Identity

- Case Studies of Brand Identity Evolution

- Conclusion: Why Brand Identity Matters

12.Working with Clients: From Brief to Design

- What to Do When Working with Clients

- How to Get the Right Brief

- The Process of Working with Clients

- Finalizing the Design

- The Psychology of Client Work

13.Mastering Design Feedback

- How to receive and process feedback

- How to handle negative or conflicting feedback

- The importance of continuous learning and adapting to feedback

- Feedback loops and client communication

- Creating a positive feedback culture

14.The Business of Graphic Design: Freelancing or Agency Work?

- Career Choice: Freelancing vs. Agency Work

- The Freelance Life: Finding Clients, Contracts, and Pricing Your Work

- How to Work in an Agency: Benefits and Drawbacks

- Practical Exercise: Building Your Professional Portfolio and Client Acquisition Strategy

- The Psychology of Client Work

- Time Management and Working with Deadlines

15.Digital vs. Print Design: Understanding the Difference

- Key differences between digital and print design

• Preparing files for print: resolution, color mode, and bleed

• How brands adapt designs for digital and print platforms: Mailchimp, Glossier, Everlane, Patagonia, Warby Parker

16.Moving Forward: Your Next Steps

• How to evaluate your progress and build a portfolio.

• Where to learn more: courses, books, and online communities.

The Future of Graphic Design: Trends and Innovations

Designing with Purpose: Ethical Design and Social Responsibility

Conclusion: Embrace the Creative Adventure

Acknowledgments

Glossary

Design Resources and Networking for New Creators

Introduction

What if I told you that becoming a designer is simpler than you think? That with just a bit of curiosity, the right tools, and a clear roadmap, you could create designs that inspire, captivate, and even transform?

Every day, we're surrounded by design—logos, posters, packaging, and social media posts that catch our eye. But behind every striking visual lies a story, an idea brought to life by someone just like you.

This book isn't for seasoned professionals or art school graduates. It's for anyone who's ever thought, "Could I really do this?" The answer is: yes, you can.

Why This Guide Is Different

This isn't your typical design book filled with dry theory or overwhelming technical jargon. Instead, this guide is built for beginners—those who are taking their very first steps into design.

What makes this book unique?

1.It's Practical: Each chapter focuses on hands-on skills you can use right away.

2.It's Accessible: No need for fancy tools or years of training. We'll show you how to start with what you have.

3.It's Inspiring: You'll learn from real-world examples, creative exercises, and stories of designers who started just like you.

This book takes you step by step, from understanding the basics of design to creating your own projects. Along the way, you'll discover your unique style, build confidence in your skills, and create work you're proud of.

My Journey (and Why It Matters)

For years, I believed graphic design wasn't for me. I thought you had to be born with some kind of magical artistic talent to succeed. The truth? I hadn't drawn anything since childhood. For 25 years, I ignored the creative side of myself, thinking I wasn't "good enough" to try.

Then, one day, I decided to give it a shot. Armed with an iPad, a few beginner-friendly tools, and a ton of self-doubt, I dove in. To my surprise, the designs I created weren't perfect, but they were mine. Each one taught me something new, and the more I practiced, the better I got.

I'll never forget the moment I saw my first design out in the world. It was a logo I had created for a small local brand, and one day, scrolling through Instagram, I spotted it. That feeling was unforgettable—a mix of pride, excitement, and disbelief. I couldn't believe something I had made was out there, representing a real business, connecting with people.

It was then that I realized design isn't about perfection—it's about communication, creativity, and solving problems in a way that resonates with others. It's about taking an idea and turning it into something others can see, feel, and connect with.

If I could start from scratch and find my way, so can you. And I'm here to guide you through every step of the process.

What You'll Learn

By the time you finish this book, you'll know how to:

•Take your very first steps in graphic design, even if you're starting from zero.

•Navigate beginner-friendly tools like Procreate, Canva, and Illustrator without feeling overwhelmed.

•Focus on what truly matters for beginners—choosing the right projects, using simple shapes, and understanding basic design principles.

•Avoid common mistakes that many new designers make.

•Create designs that communicate effectively, even with minimal experience.

Most importantly, you'll gain the clarity and confidence to know exactly where to start and how to keep moving forward.

Your Journey Starts Now

Graphic design is more than just a skill—it's a way to bring your ideas to life, solve problems creatively, and express yourself in ways words alone can't. Whether you're here to explore a new hobby, launch a career, or simply try something new, this book is your starting point.

So grab your tools, clear your workspace, and let's get started. From zero to design hero—it's time to unleash your creativity and take the first step into this exciting world.

Chapter 1

What Is Graphic Design?

Take a moment to look around. How many designs do you see? Maybe it's the logo on your coffee cup, the bright colors of a sale poster, or the clean layout of your favorite app. These aren't just random visuals—they're examples of graphic design shaping the way we interact with the world.

The Simple Truth About Graphic Design

At its core, graphic design is about communication. It's taking ideas and turning them into visuals that people can see, feel, and understand. It could be a bright yellow sale sign that screams, "Look at me!" or a calming green logo that says, "You can trust us."

Think about a world without graphic design. No logos to identify brands, no posters to advertise events, no packaging to catch your eye. Everything would be plain, boring, and mharder to navigate. Design doesn't just add beauty—it adds meaning.

Why Does Graphic Design Matter?

Graphic design isn't just decoration; it's a tool that helps us connect with people. A good design can:

1.Grab Attention.

Imagine scrolling through Instagram. What makes you pause? A bold ad, a catchy color scheme, or a clever layout. That's graphic design doing its job.

2.Build Trust.

A professional-looking design makes us feel confident about a brand or product. On the other hand, a messy logo or confusing flyer can have the opposite effect.

3.Tell a Story.

Great design isn't just pretty—it communicates emotions and values. Think about Apple's sleek, minimal designs. They don't just look modern; they tell you the brand is innovative and cutting-edge.

4.Influence Decisions.

Whether it's a colorful packaging or an elegant website, design can subtly guide your choices.

Where Do We See Graphic Design?

You don't need to look far to see the impact of graphic design. It's everywhere around us, in ways you might not even realize:

1.Logos: Think about Nike's swoosh or Starbucks' mermaid. These simple designs are instantly recognizable and carry powerful meanings.

2.Packaging: Have you ever bought a product just because the box looked great? Designers carefully craft packaging to grab your attention and tell you something about the product.

3.Websites and Apps: The colors, fonts, and layouts of your favorite apps aren't accidental—they're designed to make you feel something or act in a certain way.

4.Posters and Flyers: From concert ads to community events, posters are designed to grab attention and deliver a message quickly.

5.Social Media Posts: All those beautiful Instagram graphics? Someone carefully planned every font, color, and image to make them share-worthy.

A Quick Look at the History of Graphic Design

Graphic design has been around longer than you think. Here's a quick timeline of how it evolved:

1.The Earliest Days: Think back to cave paintings—those were some of the first attempts at visual storytelling.

2.The Printing Revolution: In the 1400s, the printing press made it possible to mass-produce books and visuals. Design became more about communication than decoration.

3.Modern Design Movements: In the 20th century, schools like Bauhaus taught designers to focus on simplicity and functionality.

4.The Digital Era: Today, tools like Procreate, Canva, and Adobe have made design accessible to anyone with a creative spark.

What Graphic Design Is Not

There are a lot of myths about graphic design. Let's clear a few of them up:

•It's not just for artists. You don't need to be Picasso to create something amazing. Many of the best designs start with simple shapes and ideas.

•It's not just about looking pretty. Design is about solving problems and sharing messages.

•It's not about being perfect. Some of the best designs come from experimenting and trying new things.

Real-Life Example: The Nike Logo

Did you know the Nike logo, one of the most iconic in the world, was designed by a student? Carolyn Davidson created the swoosh in 1971 for just $35. It's a simple curve, but it represents movement, energy, and speed. Today, it's a global symbol of athleticism and perseverance. This proves that great design doesn't have to be complicated—it just needs to connect with people.

Your First Steps Into Graphic Design

If you've made it this far, congratulations—you're already on your way to becoming a designer! Here's how to get started:

1.Notice the World Around You:

Look at the logos, posters, and packaging you see every day. Ask yourself:

- What makes this design effective?

- How do the colors and shapes make me feel?

- What message is it sending?

2.Start Small:

Begin with simple projects, like creating a logo or designing a social media post. Don't aim for perfection—just have fun and experiment.

3.Use Beginner-Friendly Tools:

Apps like Procreate or Canva are perfect for trying out your first designs. They're intuitive and have plenty of tutorials to guide you.

4.Keep Practicing:

The more you create, the more confident you'll become. Even if your first designs feel rough, remember: every designer starts somewhere.

Key Takeaways

1.Graphic design is all around us. From logos to Instagram posts, it shapes how we see the world.

2.It's about communication, not decoration. Good design tells a story and connects with people.

3.You don't need to be perfect to get started. With a bit of curiosity and some practice, anyone can become a designer.

Practical Exercise:

Take a look at the logos around you. Pick your favorite and ask yourself:

•What makes it stand out?

•How do the colors, fonts, and shapes work together?

•Could you design something similar with simple tools?

Chapter 2

Tools of the Trade

So, you've decided to explore the world of graphic design—great choice! But let's be honest: starting anything new can feel a bit overwhelming. What tools do you need? Is it going to cost a fortune? And how do you even begin?

Relax. The good news is that graphic design doesn't require a fancy studio or expensive gadgets. You just need a few basics, a sprinkle of curiosity, and the courage to start. Let's break it down.

What You Need to Get Started

To begin your graphic design journey, you need three essentials:

1.A Device:

•The most popular choice is an iPad. Lightweight, intuitive, and packed with incredible design apps like Procreate, it's a favorite among beginners and pros alike.

•No iPad? No problem. A laptop or desktop computer works just as well. You can even try a budget-friendly graphics tablet like a Wacom, which pairs with most computers.

2.Software:

•Think of software as your creative playground. Here are some great options:

•Procreate: Perfect for hand-drawn illustrations and sketches. It's simple to use, yet powerful enough for professional results.

•Canva: Ideal for quick, polished designs. Need a poster, Instagram post, or presentation? Canva's got you covered with drag-and-drop simplicity.

•Adobe Photoshop: The king of versatility. It's a bit more advanced but worth exploring if you want to dive deep into design.

3.Your Creativity:

•Here's the thing: no tool can create without your imagination. Creativity is what turns basic shapes into stunning designs. And trust me, you've got more creativity than you think.

Motivational Note:

"Don't get hung up on having the 'perfect' tools. Start with what you have. Even the best designers began with basic setups—they just made the most of them."

A Comparison of Software Options for Beginners

Choosing the right tool can feel like choosing a dessert at a buffet—so many great options!
Here's a quick cheat sheet to help you decide:

Software	Best For	Why It's Great	What to Watch Out For
Procreate	Illustrations, digital art	Intuitive, great for beginners	iPad only
Canva	Social media, quick designs	Easy to use, lots of templates	Limited customization for advanced needs
Adobe Photoshop	Photo editing, advanced design	Powerful, industry standard	Steep learning curve, subscription-based
Affinity Designer	Logo design, vector graphics	One-time payment, professional features	Less intuitive for beginners
Figma	UI/UX design, team collaboration	Free for personal use, cloud-based	Needs internet connection

Practical Tips for Setting Up Your Workspace

You don't need a Pinterest-perfect desk to start designing, but a well-organized workspace
can boost your productivity and creativity. Here's how to set up your ideal space:

1.Find Your Spot:

•Choose a quiet area where you can focus.

•Your desk doesn't have to be huge, but it should have enough space for your device, stylus, and maybe a cup of coffee.

2.Get the Lighting Right:

•Natural light is best, but if that's not an option, invest in a good desk lamp. Warm light reduces eye strain.

3.Stay Comfortable:

•A supportive chair is a game-changer. Your back will thank you after hours of designing.

4.Organize Your Tech:

•Use cable organizers to keep your desk tidy. A messy workspace can distract from your creativity.

5.Digital Organization:

•Create folders for your projects and save your work regularly. Cloud storage like Google Drive or Dropbox is a lifesaver if your computer ever crashes.

Motivational Note:

"A well-organized space isn't just about looking good—it's about setting the stage for your creativity to shine."

Exercise: Get Comfortable With Your Tools

Let's get hands-on! This simple exercise will help you familiarize yourself with your tools:

1.Open your chosen software (Procreate, Canva, or Photoshop).

2.Create a blank canvas.

•Canva: Choose a template for a social media post.

•Procreate/Photoshop: Set up a custom canvas (1080x1080 px is perfect).

3.Try these steps:

•Add a background color.

•Draw simple shapes (a circle, rectangle, or triangle).

•Add text: write your name and experiment with different fonts.

4.Save your work.

"See? You just created your first design. It's simple, but it's yours. Every great designer starts here."

Real-Life Example: Canva in Action

Meet Sarah. She's a small business owner who wanted to create Instagram posts to promote her products but had no idea where to start. After downloading Canva, she picked a free template, added her brand colors, and typed her slogan. Within an hour, she had a professional-looking post ready to share.

Sarah's confidence grew, and now she designs all her social media posts herself.

Key Takeaway:

"The right tool can make all the difference, but it's your creativity that makes it shine."

Key Takeaways

•You don't need to spend a fortune—start with the basics: a device, software, and your imagination.

•Explore tools like Procreate, Canva, and Photoshop, and find what feels right for you.

•A well-organized workspace inspires creativity and helps you stay focused.

•Practice every day. Small steps lead to big progress.

Chapter 3

Building Blocks: Shapes, Lines, and Textures

Every masterpiece starts with simple elements. In graphic design, these elements—shapes, lines, and textures—are the building blocks that form the foundation of any great design. They may seem basic, but when used thoughtfully, they can bring your ideas to life in ways that captivate and inspire.

Think of these elements as the Lego pieces of design. On their own, they're just shapes, but when combined with creativity, they can build castles, rockets, or anything else your imagination dreams up.

Shapes: The Backbone of Design

Shapes are everywhere in design. They create structure, guide the viewer's eye, and set the tone for your message. Even the most complex designs you admire start with a simple circle or square.

1.Geometric Shapes:

•These are the classic building blocks: circles, squares, rectangles, and triangles.

•*What they convey:*

•Circles feel harmonious and inviting. Ever notice how most social media profile pictures are circular? It's no accident—it's about making people feel comfortable.

•Squares and rectangles are solid and trustworthy. That's why so many business cards and posters rely on these shapes.

•Triangles suggest movement and energy. They're perfect for dynamic, edgy designs.

Examples in the real world:

•Target's logo uses a simple circle to create instant recognition.

•The Play button on YouTube? A triangle—it's a shape that screams action!

2.Organic Shapes:

•These are freeform, irregular shapes inspired by nature.

•*What they convey:*

•They feel soft, approachable, and spontaneous, often adding a human touch to designs.

•Look at logos for eco-friendly brands—they often use leaves or abstract organic shapes to represent nature.

3.Abstract Shapes:

•Simplified representations of concepts, often used to communicate ideas visually.

Examples:

•A heart icon for love, a lightning bolt for energy, or a star for success.

Motivational Note:

"Don't overthink it. Start with one shape and build from there. The simplest designs are often the most memorable."

Lines: Small but Mighty

Lines are the invisible threads that hold your design together. They're subtle but incredibly powerful tools that can make or break a composition.

1.Structuring Your Design:

•Lines create boundaries and separate sections, making your layout easy to follow.

Example: Think of a website menu where clean dividers separate categories. Without those lines, everything would blur together.

2.Guiding the Eye:

•Leading lines naturally draw attention to the focal point of your design.

Example: Have you seen a flyer where arrows point to a QR code or a sale price? That's no accident—it's smart design.

3.Setting the Mood:

•Straight lines are stable and formal. That's why corporate reports use them.

•Curved lines are playful and dynamic, perfect for kids' brands or creative projects.

•Thick lines feel bold, while thin lines are elegant.

Inspirational Thought:

"A single line can transform a blank canvas into a story. Think of it as the first stroke of your masterpiece."

Textures: The Secret to Depth

Textures bring a design to life. They can make a flat image feel tactile, rich, and real.

1.Subtle Background Textures:

•A paper-like texture or soft gradient can make your background feel more polished without distracting from the main elements.

Example: Vintage posters often use grainy textures to evoke nostalgia.

2.Highlighting Key Elements:

•Add texture to specific areas, like a title or a shape, to draw attention.

Example: Think of a business card with embossed text—it feels luxurious, even though it's just a simple texture.

3.Combining Textures Wisely:

•Keep it balanced. Too many textures can overwhelm your audience.

Motivational Note:

"Textures aren't just for decoration—they tell a story. A rough texture can evoke strength, while a soft one feels welcoming."

Practical Exercise: Create a Balanced Composition

Ready to test your skills? Let's create a simple yet striking design using just circles and lines.

Objective:

Design a balanced composition that feels harmonious and dynamic.

Steps:

1.Open your design software (Procreate, Canva, or Photoshop).

2.Create a blank canvas.

•Recommended size: 1080x1080 px.

3.Add a large circle in the center of your canvas.

4.Use lines to connect the circle to other areas of the canvas.

•Experiment with different line styles: solid, dashed, or dotted.

5.Add smaller circles around the main one.

•Play with sizes, colors, and spacing to create a sense of balance.

6.Adjust until the composition feels complete.

Inspirational Example:

"The London Underground map is a masterpiece made of just lines and circles. It's proof that simplicity can be powerful."

Real-Life Example: The Power of Simplicity

Think about Apple's logo. It's just a simple shape—a bitten apple. Yet it's one of the most recognizable symbols in the world. Why? Because it's clean, intentional, and perfectly balanced.

Another example: IKEA's product manuals. They rely entirely on shapes and lines to communicate instructions. No words needed—just effective visual design.

Motivational Note:

"Every design starts with a single shape, line, or texture. The magic happens when you bring them together with purpose."

Key Takeaways

•Shapes: Geometric shapes provide structure, organic shapes add spontaneity, and abstract shapes communicate ideas.

•Lines: Guide attention, define spaces, and set the mood.

•Textures: Bring depth and tactile quality to flat designs.

•Practice: Start with simple compositions and build from there.

Chapter 4

The Power of Color

Imagine walking into a room painted a deep, calming blue. Now picture the same room painted bright, fiery red. Feels completely different, right? That's the power of color in action.

In graphic design, color isn't just decoration—it's communication. It grabs attention, sets the mood, and even influences our decisions in ways we don't always realize. Let's explore how you can harness the power of color to create designs that connect, inspire, and leave a lasting impression.

How Colors Influence Emotions and Decisions

Colors speak a universal language. They evoke emotions, shape perceptions, and even trigger memories. Let's explore not only individual colors but also how they work together to amplify your message.

1.Contrasting Colors:

•Contrasts grab attention by creating energy and focus.

Example: Red and green are opposites on the color wheel, making them perfect for festive, high-energy designs.

2.Analogous Colors:

•These are colors next to each other on the wheel (like blue and green). They create a sense of harmony and unity.

Example: Think of nature—blue skies blending into green fields.

3.Monochromatic Colors:

•Using different shades of a single color creates an elegant and cohesive look.

Example: A brand that uses varying shades of blue communicates trust and sophistication without overwhelming the viewer.

4.Warm vs. Cool Colors:

•Warm colors (reds, yellows, oranges) feel energetic and welcoming.

•Cool colors (blues, greens, purples) feel calming and professional.

Pro Tip:

"When choosing colors, think of the story you're telling. Are you creating a sense of urgency or tranquility? Your palette should reflect that."

Motivational Story: Turning Ideas into Impact with Color

Meet Julia. She was a freelance designer tasked with creating a logo for a small organic skincare brand. The client wanted the logo to feel fresh, luxurious, and eco-friendly. Julia started with greens for nature and growth but struggled to find the right balance.

Then she added a soft gold accent. Suddenly, the logo came to life, blending green's natural appeal with gold's luxurious touch. When the logo launched, the brand's sales doubled in just six months, and Julia became the client's go-to designer for future projects.

Lesson Learned:

"The right color combination can do more than make something look good—it can transform perceptions and build success."

Real-Life Examples of Color in Branding

1.McDonald's:

•Colors: Red and yellow.

•Why It Works: Red triggers excitement and appetite, while yellow feels cheerful and welcoming. Combined, they create an inviting atmosphere that says, "Come eat and enjoy!"

2.Tiffany & Co.:

•Colors: Signature Tiffany Blue.

•Why It Works: This exclusive shade of blue is associated with elegance, luxury, and timeless style. It's so iconic that people refer to it as "Tiffany Blue."

3.Coca-Cola:

•Colors: Bold red.

•Why It Works: Red is exciting, vibrant, and celebratory—perfect for Coca-Cola's message of happiness and sharing moments.

4.Starbucks:

•Colors: Green.

•Why It Works: Green represents growth, calmness, and sustainability—values that align perfectly with Starbucks' eco-friendly mission.

5.Google:

•Colors: Red, blue, green, and yellow.

•Why It Works: The playful combination of colors reflects Google's innovative, creative, and accessible brand identity.

Practical Exercise: Create a Color Palette for an Imaginary Brand

Let's put theory into practice! In this exercise, you'll create a color palette for a fictional brand.

Objective:

Design a color palette that captures the personality and goals of your imaginary brand.

Steps:

1.Choose a Brand Type:

•Is it a cozy coffee shop, a modern tech startup, or a playful toy store?

Example: A coffee shop might feel warm and inviting, while a tech startup might feel innovative and trustworthy.

2.Define the Brand's Personality:

•Ask yourself:

•Should the brand feel bold and energetic, or calm and professional?

•What emotions do you want customers to feel?

3.Select Colors:

•Pick 2-3 primary colors and 1-2 accent colors.

Example for a toy store:

•Primary colors: Bright red (excitement), Yellow (happiness).

•Accent color: Blue (trust).

4.Create a Mockup:

•Apply your palette to a simple logo, business card, or social media header.

5.Test and Refine:

•Look at your design on different devices. Does it evoke the emotions you intended?

Inspirational Note:

"Every brand tells a story, and colors are your narrator. Make your story unforgettable."

Key Takeaways

•Colors are a powerful tool to evoke emotions and influence decisions.

•Contrasts create energy, analogous colors build harmony, and monochromatic palettes offer   elegance.

•Successful brands use color intentionally to communicate their identity.

•Your choice of colors should align with your brand's personality and goals.

•Practice by experimenting with color palettes to understand their impact.

Chapter 5

Fonts and Typography ;)

Typography is more than just words on a page—it's the voice of your design. It can whisper elegance, shout excitement, or speak with calm authority. A well-chosen font doesn't just look good; it makes your message unforgettable.

Let's explore the power of fonts and how you can use them to elevate your designs.

Choosing and Pairing Fonts Effectively

Fonts are like personalities—they have their own character, mood, and style. Choosing the right one is like picking the perfect person to represent your idea.

1.Know Your Font Categories:

•Serif Fonts:

•These fonts have little "feet" or decorative strokes.

Example: Times New Roman for tradition, Georgia for modernity with a classic twist.

•Sans-Serif Fonts:

•Clean, minimalist fonts without decorative strokes.

Example: Helvetica for timeless professionalism, Arial for simplicity.

•Script Fonts:

•Flowing, elegant fonts that mimic handwriting.

Example: Great Vibes for sophistication, Pacifico for a playful tone.

•Display Fonts:

•Bold and unique, designed for headlines or logos.

Example: Impact for strength, Lobster for vintage flair.

2.Pair Fonts Like a Pro:

•Use contrasting styles to create balance.

Example: Pair a bold sans-serif (like Futura) with a refined serif (like Baskerville).

•Stick to two fonts per design to avoid clutter.

Netflix's logo uses a bold, clean sans-serif font to communicate modernity and accessibility. Meanwhile, Vogue's iconic serif font evokes timeless elegance and luxury.

Pro Tip:

"Choosing fonts isn't just about aesthetics—it's about making your message resonate."

The Transformative Power of Typography

Fonts aren't just tools; they're storytellers. Imagine these scenarios:

1.The Wrong Font:

•A wedding invitation in Comic Sans.

•A legal document in Papyrus.

•They feel out of place, don't they?

2.The Right Font:

•A bold sans-serif for a tech startup screams innovation.

•A flowing script for a luxury brand whispers sophistication.

•Fonts can make or break the tone of your message.

Motivational Story:

Sarah, a junior designer, once worked on a project for a local coffee shop. Her first draft looked good, but something was missing. After swapping a generic sans-serif font for a vintage serif, the design transformed. The new font captured the shop's cozy, nostalgic vibe and resonated with customers. The shop's sales grew, and Sarah's career took off.

Lesson:

"Typography isn't just about looking good—it's about feeling right."

Tips to Avoid Common Typography Mistakes

Even experienced designers stumble over typography. Here's how to avoid common traps:

1.Don't Stretch or Distort Fonts:

•Proportional scaling keeps your fonts professional and readable.

2.Limit Font Choices:

•Mixing too many fonts creates visual noise. Stick to 2-3 per project.

3.Perfect Your Spacing:

•Adjust kerning (space between letters) for better readability.

•Use proper leading (space between lines) to keep your text inviting.

4.Avoid Clichés:

•Skip overused fonts like Comic Sans or Papyrus. Instead, explore free font libraries like Google Fonts for fresh alternatives.

Pro Tip:

"Typography is an art form—treat it with care, and your designs will thank you."

Practical Exercise: Design a Poster Using Two Contrasting Fonts

Ready to flex your typography skills? Here's a fun exercise to help you master font pairing and layout.

Objective:

Design an eye-catching poster using only two contrasting fonts.

Steps:

1.Pick a Theme:

•Is it a concert? A book launch? A motivational quote? Choose your subject.

2.Select Two Fonts:

•Use contrast for impact:

Example: Pair a strong sans-serif (like Bebas Neue) with a delicate script (like Dancing Script).

3.Create a Layout:

•Use the bold font for the headline to grab attention.

•Place supporting text (dates, location) in the second font.

4.Experiment with Spacing and Alignment:

•Adjust kerning and leading to balance the composition.

5.Add Finishing Touches:

•Incorporate shapes, colors, or subtle textures to enhance your design without overpowering the fonts.

Bonus Challenge:

Create a second version of your poster, swapping the fonts' roles. Notice how it changes the overall feel?

Key Takeaways

•Fonts aren't just text—they're personalities. Choose ones that fit your design's mood and message.

•Pair contrasting fonts for balance and interest.

•Avoid common typography mistakes like stretching fonts or overcrowding your designs.

•Practice by creating layouts that let typography shine as the main element.

Chapter 6

How to Create Your First Logo

Logos are everywhere—on your coffee cup, on the apps you use daily, and even on your sneakers. They're more than just symbols; they're the face of a brand. A good logo is simple yet memorable, leaving a lasting impression. But how do you create one that stands out?

In this chapter, we'll explore what makes a logo effective, take you through the process of designing one, and dive into the stories behind some of the most unique and interesting logos in the world. Let's get started.

What Makes a Logo Effective

Creating a logo might seem simple, but designing one that's truly effective requires thought and intention. Here are the key ingredients:

1.Simplicity:

•A simple logo is easy to recognize and remember. Think of the WWF panda—it's clean, emotional, and instantly recognizable.

2.Relevance:

•Your logo should reflect your brand's personality and values.

Example: The Dropbox logo features a simple, open box, symbolizing storage and accessibility.

3.Versatility:

•A great logo works across all mediums—business cards, websites, and billboards. It should look good in black and white as well as color.

4.Memorability:

•Can people recall your logo after seeing it once? A strong, unique design ensures your brand sticks in their mind.

Example: The negative space in the FedEx logo forms a hidden arrow, subtly reinforcing the brand's focus on speed and precision.

5.Timelessness:

•Avoid trends that might feel outdated in a few years. A timeless logo ensures longevity.

Example: Chanel's interlocking "C" logo has remained elegant and iconic for decades.

Fun Fact:

"FedEx's arrow wasn't noticed by the general public until years after its creation, proving that subtlety can be powerful."

Pro Tip:

"Before sketching, think about your brand's story. What message should your logo convey?"

Step-by-Step Guide to Creating a Logo

Designing your first logo might feel overwhelming, but breaking it down into steps makes it manageable. Let's walk through the process:

1.Understand the Brand:

•Ask key questions:

•What is the brand's mission?

•Who is the target audience?

•What emotions should the logo evoke?

2.Research and Gather Inspiration:

•Look at logos from similar industries. What works, and what doesn't?

•Use platforms like Pinterest or Behance to collect examples that inspire you.

3.Sketch Ideas:

•Start with pen and paper. Don't worry about perfection—this is the brainstorming phase.

•Experiment with shapes, symbols, and text layouts.

4.Choose Fonts and Colors:

•Pick fonts and colors that reflect the brand's personality.

Example: A modern tech startup might use a sleek sans-serif font and cool tones, while a bakery might choose a script font with warm, pastel colors.

5.Design Digitally:

•Use tools like Procreate, Canva, or Adobe Illustrator to create a polished version of your logo.

6.Test and Refine:

•See how your logo looks in different sizes and formats.

•Get feedback from friends, colleagues, or potential users.

Fun Fact:

"The WWF panda logo was designed to save costs—it's simple, requires no color, and conveys the organization's mission to protect wildlife."

Real-Life Case Studies: WWF, Dropbox, and FedEx

1.WWF (World Wildlife Fund):

•The Panda: Designed in 1961, it's simple, memorable, and universal.

•Why It Works: The black-and-white design saves printing costs and conveys an emotional connection to wildlife.

2.Dropbox:

•The Open Box: The logo symbolizes storage and sharing.

•Why It Works: Its simplicity makes it versatile across digital platforms while staying relevant to the brand's mission.

3.FedEx:

•The Hidden Arrow: The negative space between the "E" and "x" forms an arrow, symbolizing speed and efficiency.

•Why It Works: The design is clever, subtle, and instantly recognizable once you notice the arrow.

Motivational Note:

"Great logos don't need to shout—they let their design speak for them. Your logo can be powerful, even with the simplest concept."

Practical Exercise: Design a Logo for a Fictional Coffee Shop

Let's put your skills to the test! Imagine you're designing a logo for a cozy, modern coffee shop called "Brew Haven."

Objective:

Create a simple, versatile logo that reflects the shop's friendly and inviting atmosphere.

Steps:

1.Define the Brand Personality:

•Think cozy, modern, and approachable.

2.Sketch Ideas:

•Experiment with coffee-related symbols like a cup, bean, or steam.

•Play with shapes (circles for warmth, sharp lines for modernity).

3.Pick Fonts and Colors:

•Fonts: Try a rounded sans-serif for a friendly vibe or a handwritten script for warmth.

•Colors: Use rich browns, creams, and a splash of green to represent freshness.

4.Design Digitally:

•Create your final version using design software.

5.Test Your Logo:

•Place it on a mockup (coffee cups, menus, or signs) to see how it looks in real life.

Bonus Challenge:

Design a second version of the logo in black and white. This helps ensure your logo works in any context.

Key Takeaways

•Effective logos are simple, relevant, versatile, memorable, and timeless.

•A well-designed logo tells a brand's story and connects emotionally with its audience.

•Practice by creating logos for fictional brands to sharpen your skills.

•Even subtle elements, like the arrow in FedEx or the panda in WWF, can make your logo unforgettable.

Chapter 7

Creating Visual Hierarchy

What is Visual Hierarchy?

Visual hierarchy is the arrangement or presentation of design elements in a way that prioritizes certain information and guides the viewer's attention naturally. It's the art of directing the viewer's eye to the most important parts of the design first, then leading them through the other elements in a clear and intuitive flow. Whether you're working on a poster, a website, a magazine spread, or a social media post, visual hierarchy is crucial for creating designs that are not only visually engaging but also effective in communicating a message.

At its core, visual hierarchy is a design tool that leverages the relationship between elements in your layout to help your audience focus on what matters. It helps create order and ensures that your design isn't overwhelming or confusing to the viewer. It's about creating a logical flow of information that makes the experience of engaging with the design seamless.

Fundamentals of Visual Hierarchy

To create an effective visual hierarchy, you need to consider several principles, each of which plays a crucial role in how your design will be perceived:

1.Size and Scale

•Larger elements naturally attract more attention. When you increase the size of an element, it signals to the viewer that it is more important. The larger the element, the more focus it demands. This is why headers, main images, and primary call-to-action buttons are typically larger than the rest of the content in your design.

Example:

In an advertisement for a fashion brand, the main image of the product will likely be the largest element, followed by the headline (like a discount offer), then the smaller text describing features or other details.

Real-Life Case Study:

Patagonia, the outdoor clothing brand, uses large, bold typography for their environmental slogans like "We're in business to save our home planet." The message is the first thing that grabs your attention, while smaller product images follow to showcase the actual goods.

2.Color

•Colors have the power to direct attention and can enhance the impact of the design. Bright colors or high contrast colors will catch the eye first, while muted tones tend to fade into the background. By using color strategically, you can emphasize key elements in your design and ensure that important messages stand out.

Example:

Coca-Cola uses its signature red and white color scheme to make its logo and key message pop, creating a sense of excitement and energy. Meanwhile, Tiffany & Co. uses their iconic blue to exude luxury and sophistication, guiding the viewer to feel exclusivity when engaging with the brand.

Real-Life Case Study:

Spotify uses vibrant green and black to create contrast and energy. The vibrant green grabs attention immediately, particularly in call-to-action buttons like "Play" or "Get Started." The bold contrast against a dark background makes these buttons easy to spot.

Practical Tip:

Use contrast in colors to separate key areas of the design. High contrast areas draw attention quickly, while more subdued colors can indicate secondary information.

3.Typography

•Typography is one of the most effective tools for controlling visual hierarchy. The size, weight, and style of fonts can differentiate the importance of each piece of text. Bold, large fonts often indicate something of greater importance, like a headline or primary message, while smaller, lighter fonts are used for supporting information.

Example:

Nike uses bold, clean typography for their primary slogan "Just Do It," making it the most prominent part of the design. Meanwhile, product details and other messaging are presented in a more understated font size, making them secondary to the brand message.

Real-Life Case Study:

The New York Times uses strong typography to emphasize headlines and subheadings. The typefaces chosen convey authority and seriousness, while lighter fonts for article text make the content easily readable. Their use of size and weight helps lead the reader's eye through the content smoothly.

Practical Tip:

Use a maximum of two or three fonts to maintain consistency and clarity in your design. Consider pairing a bold font for headlines with a lighter, simpler font for body text.

4.Spacing and Alignment

•Spacing between elements is another critical tool in establishing hierarchy. Proper spacing allows each element to breathe and ensures clarity. Too little space between items can create a cluttered design, while ample spacing can help the viewer process information at a comfortable pace.

Example:

Apple's website has a minimalist design with a lot of negative space. This use of space makes the product and key messaging stand out without overwhelming the viewer. The careful alignment and ample spacing between sections guide the user's eyes from one element to the next.

Real-Life Case Study:

Dropbox uses clear, generous white space to make their website feel clean and modern. Their homepage focuses on the central action—signing up or logging in—while other elements are neatly aligned with consistent spacing to avoid overwhelming the user.

Practical Tip:

Be mindful of white space (or negative space). It helps to isolate key elements and makes your design feel clean and accessible.

5.Contrast

•Contrast involves using differences in size, color, shape, and other design elements to create emphasis. High contrast areas will naturally grab attention, helping to establish clear focal points within your design.

Example:

Spotify uses dark backgrounds to set off bright, contrasting buttons and icons. This makes it easy for users to find what they're looking for and provides a simple, clean interface that doesn't overwhelm.

Real-Life Case Study:

Target uses high contrast between its red logo and the white background, ensuring that the brand stands out immediately. This use of bold contrast drives the viewer's attention to the most important visual elements first, like their deals and products.

Practical Tip:

Experiment with contrast not just in color, but in size, shape, and positioning. For example, a large white button on a dark background will naturally draw attention.

How to Apply Visual Hierarchy in Your Designs

To put visual hierarchy into practice, follow these steps:

1.Start with the Most Important Information

Identify the core message of your design. Is it the product you're selling, the event you're promoting, or a special offer? This should be the most prominent element on the page. Use size, color, and typography to make sure this element stands out from the rest of the content.

2.Organize Supporting Information

After highlighting the most important part of the design, focus on the secondary elements. This could include additional details like dates, prices, descriptions, or supplementary features. Use smaller fonts, lighter colors, or placement further down the page to indicate that this information is of lesser importance.

3.Use Clear Layouts to Guide the Eye

A good layout will guide the viewer's eye through the design in a natural flow. Place elements in a way that creates an intuitive path for the viewer's eye, making it easy to process information in a logical sequence.

4.Test Your Design

Once you've arranged your design, step back and assess the flow of information. Does the most important information stand out? Is there any area that feels too cluttered or difficult to follow? Test with others to ensure that your hierarchy makes sense to different people.

Examples of How Brands Use Visual Hierarchy

1.Nike:

The Nike website is an excellent example of how visual hierarchy directs attention. The main visual—the product—is placed front and center, with bold typography for the "Just Do It" slogan. The rest of the text is neatly organized in smaller fonts, guiding the viewer's eye from most important to least important information.

2.McDonald's:

McDonald's uses large, bold typography and bright colors to highlight their latest offers or promotions. The red and yellow color scheme immediately grabs attention, while secondary information (like nutritional info or store hours) is placed in a less prominent position.

3.Airbnb:

Airbnb uses a clean, simple layout that relies on large images and clear calls-to-action. The "Search" button is the largest element on the page, followed by other navigation options, ensuring users know exactly what action to take next.

4.Patagonia:

Patagonia's ads use large, impactful headlines paired with stunning images to grab attention, emphasizing their environmental messages. The typography is clean and straightforward, with secondary details about the products being smaller and more subdued, allowing the viewer to focus on the bigger picture.

5.The New York Times:

The New York Times uses bold headlines and strategic use of whitespace to highlight key stories while guiding the reader's attention smoothly through articles and ads. The typography and layout ensure clarity and prioritization of content, ensuring a positive reading experience.

Practical Exercise

Create a poster for a fictional event using the principles of visual hierarchy. Decide on your most important piece of information (e.g., event name, time, location) and make it the most prominent. Use size, color, typography, and spacing to organize your content, ensuring that the viewer's eye naturally flows from the most important to the least important details. Once completed, test your design by asking others to review it and provide feedback.

Conclusion

Mastering visual hierarchy is essential for creating designs that are not only aesthetically pleasing but also functional and easy to understand. By controlling how viewers process information, you can guide their attention and ensure they focus on the most important aspects of your design. Whether you're working on a website, a flyer, or a social media post, applying these principles will help you create more effective and professional designs that engage and communicate effectively with your audience.

Chapter 8

Patterns and Textures

Patterns and textures are like the unsung heroes of design. They can add depth, personality, and style to anything—from product packaging to social media graphics. But how do you create patterns that look professional and textures that elevate your designs rather than overwhelm them?

Let's dive into the art of patterns and textures, exploring how to create them, when to use them, and how they can transform your designs.

How to Create Repeating Patterns

Repeating patterns are everywhere: on wrapping paper, fabric, wallpaper, and even websites. The secret to a great repeating pattern lies in its ability to flow seamlessly. Here's how you can create one:

1.Start with a Simple Motif:

•Choose a single element as your base, like a flower, a geometric shape, or even a hand-drawn doodle.

2.Arrange the Motif Strategically:

•Use a grid or offset layout to arrange your motif.

•Experiment with rotation, scaling, and spacing to create visual interest.

3.Test for Seamlessness:

•Ensure your pattern repeats without visible gaps or misalignments.

•Most design tools like Adobe Illustrator or Procreate have built-in features for testing seamless patterns.

4.Add Color:

•Choose a color palette that complements your pattern. Start with 2-3 colors and gradually expand if needed.

Pro Tip:

"Less is more. A clean, simple pattern is often more effective than one that feels overcrowded."

Using Textures to Add Depth

Textures can transform a flat design into something tactile and engaging. But using them effectively requires balance.

1.Subtle Textures for Backgrounds:

•Use light textures like paper grain, gradients, or subtle noise to add depth without distracting from your main elements.

2.Highlighting with Bold Textures:

•Apply bolder textures, like woodgrain or metallic effects, to specific parts of your design (e.g., a logo or a border).

3.Combine Textures and Patterns Wisely:

•Avoid mixing too many textures in one design. Choose one texture to lead and keep others subtle.

Inspirational Example:

The texture of Louis Vuitton's signature monogram pattern on leather has become synonymous with exclusivity and luxury. It's not just about the look—it's about the tactile experience.

Pro Tip:

"Textures are like spices—use just enough to enhance, but not so much that they overwhelm."

Adding Digital Tools to Your Workflow

Technology has made creating patterns and textures easier than ever. Here are some tools that can simplify the process:

1.Adobe Illustrator:

•Use the "Pattern Maker" feature to create seamless designs effortlessly.

2.Procreate:

•Offers brushes and templates for designing unique patterns directly on your iPad.

3.Canva:

•Perfect for beginners. You can combine shapes, colors, and textures to make quick patterns without advanced skills.

4.Affinity Designer:

•A cost-effective alternative to Adobe Illustrator, great for creating vector patterns.

Fun Fact:

"The first digital patterns were painstakingly created pixel by pixel. Today, tools like Procreate make the process as simple as a few taps on your screen."

Pro Tip:

"Experiment with different tools to find what works best for your style and workflow."

Real-Life Inspiration: Patterns That Define Brands

1.Burberry:

•The classic Burberry plaid is instantly recognizable and synonymous with luxury. Originally a lining for trench coats, it has become a global icon.

2.Louis Vuitton:

•The monogram pattern combines the founder's initials with floral motifs. It's timeless, elegant, and instantly associated with high-end fashion.

3.Starbucks:

•Starbucks often incorporates earthy, natural patterns in its packaging, reflecting the brand's eco-conscious values.

4.Marimekko:

•This Finnish brand is known for bold, colorful patterns that have made their way onto clothing, home goods, and even architecture.

Motivational Note:

"Your pattern doesn't have to be famous to make an impact. Start small, and who knows—one day, it could define a brand."

Practical Exercise: Design a Simple Pattern for a Product Package

Let's put theory into practice. Imagine you're designing a pattern for a fictional skincare brand called "Glow Naturals."

Objective:

Create a repeating pattern that reflects the brand's values of natural beauty and sustainability.

Steps:

1.Choose Your Motif:

•Think of natural elements like leaves, flowers, or water droplets.

2.Arrange the Pattern:

•Use a grid or random layout to position your motifs.

3.Select Colors:

•Opt for soft greens, earthy browns, and neutral creams to align with the brand's theme.

4.Add Texture:

•Apply a subtle paper texture or gradient to enhance the design.

5.Test Your Pattern:

•Place it on a mockup (e.g., a product box or bottle) to see how it looks in real life.

Bonus Challenge:

Create two variations of your pattern: one bold and colorful, and another minimalist and neutral. Compare how they change the brand's feel.

Motivational Note:

"Your pattern isn't just a background—it's part of the product's story. Let it speak for the brand."

Key Takeaways

•Patterns and textures add personality and depth to your designs.

•Repeating patterns should flow seamlessly and complement the design's purpose.

•Subtle textures can enhance a design without overpowering it.

•Patterns are a powerful tool for branding, extending beyond packaging to other brand elements.

•Practice by creating patterns and textures for fictional products to refine your skills.

Chapter 9

Designing for Social Media

Social media is where design meets the fast-paced, visual world of digital communication. With just a few seconds to grab someone's attention as they scroll, your design needs to be bold, clear, and visually appealing. Whether you're creating a post for Instagram, a TikTok thumbnail, or a banner for Facebook, the principles remain the same.

Let's explore the key elements of social media design, look at some effective examples, and practice creating a post that stands out.

Key Principles for Social Media Graphics

Designing for social media comes with its own set of rules. Here's how to create graphics that work:

1.Format Matters:

•Know the Dimensions: Each platform has specific dimensions for posts, stories, and ads.

•Instagram Post: 1080x1080 px (square).

•TikTok Thumbnail: 1080x1920 px (vertical).

•Facebook Cover: 1200x630 px (landscape).

•A properly sized image ensures your design looks professional and doesn't get cropped awkwardly.

2.Colors That Pop:

•Use bold, high-contrast colors to grab attention.

•Stick to your brand's color palette for consistency.

•Add a touch of vibrancy, as social media is a visually competitive space.

3.Typography for Impact:

•Use clear, readable fonts.

•Keep the text minimal—let visuals do the talking.

•Pair a bold font for headlines with a simpler font for supporting text.

4.Hierarchy and Balance:

•Make the most important element (like the headline or product) the focal point.

•Use white space strategically to avoid clutter.

Fun Fact:

"On average, users spend only 1.7 seconds looking at a piece of content on their feed. That's your window to impress!"

Pro Tip:

"Design for the scroll. Your post should be eye-catching even when seen for just a second."

Examples of Effective Social Media Designs

Let's look at how some brands have nailed their social media designs:

1.Instagram - Netflix:

•Why It Works: Netflix uses bold, minimalist designs with dramatic imagery to announce new shows. The use of high-quality visuals and sharp contrasts creates instant impact.

2.TikTok - Duolingo:

•Why It Works: Duolingo's TikTok thumbnails feature the brand's signature green owl, playful fonts, and bright colors. They align with the app's fun and approachable personality.

3.Facebook - Canva:

•Why It Works: Canva's Facebook posts often include simple, clean designs with a clear call to action. They showcase their tools while keeping the focus on user benefits.

Fun Fact:

"Red and yellow are often called 'power colors' because they naturally grab attention. That's why so many brands, from McDonald's to Netflix, use them in their designs."

The Power of Animation in Social Media

Static posts are powerful, but adding animation can take your design to the next level:

1.Use Light Animations:

•Subtle GIFs, moving text, or bouncing icons can make your design more engaging.

2.Highlight Key Information:

•Use animations to draw attention to discounts, events, or product launches.

3.Keep It Short:

•Most animations should loop seamlessly and last no more than 5-10 seconds.

Pro Tip:

"A simple animated element can turn a good post into a scroll-stopping masterpiece."

How to Adapt Designs for Different Platforms

Every social media platform has its own vibe. Adapting your designs ensures they resonate with the right audience:

1.Instagram:

•Visual storytelling is key. Use high-quality photos, bold text overlays, and creative layouts.

2.TikTok:

•Prioritize movement and personality. Even static thumbnails should hint at the energy of your video.

3.Facebook:

•Include more information, as users might spend more time reading. Balance text and visuals.

4.Pinterest:

•Focus on vertical layouts and aspirational designs. Use muted tones for a sophisticated feel.

Pro Tip:

"One design doesn't fit all. Tailor your posts to fit each platform's unique audience and format."

Practical Exercise: Create a Post for Instagram Using Simple Elements

Let's put your skills to the test. Imagine you're designing a post for a fictional fitness app called "FitNow."

Objective:

Create an engaging Instagram post that encourages users to download the app.

Steps:

1.Choose Your Format:

•Use a square canvas (1080x1080 px) to match Instagram's standard post size.

2.Pick Your Colors:

•Use vibrant, energetic colors like orange and blue to reflect the fitness theme.

3.Add Text:

•Keep the headline short and punchy: "Your Fitness Journey Starts Today!"

•Include a call to action: "Download the FitNow App for Free."

4.Incorporate Imagery:

•Use a high-quality photo of someone exercising or a graphic of fitness equipment.

5.Finish with Your Logo:

•Place the FitNow logo in the corner for branding.

6.Add Animation (Optional):

•Experiment with moving text or a pulsing "Download Now" button for added engagement.

Motivational Note:

"Your design might be the reason someone decides to take action. Make it bold, make it clear, and make it count."

Key Takeaways

•Social media design requires attention to format, colors, typography, and balance.

•Different platforms demand tailored designs to resonate with their unique audiences.

•Eye-catching colors and minimal text are key to grabbing attention in a busy feed.

•Animation and movement can significantly enhance engagement.

•Practice by creating posts for fictional brands to refine your skills.

Chapter 10

Finding Your Creative Voice

Every designer has a unique story to tell, and your creative voice is what makes your work stand out. But discovering your own style isn't always easy—it's a journey of exploration, experimentation, and sometimes even failure.

In this chapter, we'll explore how to find your creative voice, draw inspiration from others, and create designs that are authentically you.

How to Discover Your Unique Style

Your creative style is like your fingerprint—completely unique to you. Here's how to start uncovering it:

1.Experiment with Different Styles:

•Try out various design trends and techniques. You might discover that you love minimalism or thrive in vibrant, chaotic designs.

•Don't be afraid to mimic styles at first—this is a learning phase, not plagiarism.

2.Reflect on Your Influences:

•Think about the things you naturally gravitate toward—your favorite colors, patterns, or even movies and music. These influences shape your creative voice.

3.Embrace Your Background:

•Your cultural heritage, personal experiences, and hobbies can add depth to your work.

Example: A designer with a love for nature might create organic, earthy designs, while someone fascinated by technology might lean toward futuristic styles.

4.Gather Feedback:

•Share your work with friends, peers, or online communities. Honest feedback can help you see your strengths and areas for growth.

5.Create Consistently:

•The more you create, the more your style will evolve. Consistent practice is the key to uncovering your voice.

Pro Tip:

"Your unique style isn't something you find—it's something you create over time."

Fun Fact:

"Did you know that many famous designers discovered their style after experimenting with ideas they thought would fail? Sometimes, creativity comes from unexpected places."

Learning from Mistakes and Happy Accidents

Not every design you create will be a masterpiece, and that's okay. Mistakes are a natural part of the creative process and often lead to surprising breakthroughs.

1.The Unexpected Power of Accidents:

•Some of the most iconic styles started as mistakes.

Example: A designer experimenting with Photoshop accidentally created a distortion effect, which later became their signature style.

2.Embrace Imperfection:

•Don't aim for perfection—aim for progress. Your unique voice often emerges when you let go of rigid rules.

3.Learn and Adapt:

•Treat every mistake as a learning opportunity. Ask yourself, "What worked here, and what didn't?"

Motivational Note:

"Every misstep is a step toward discovering who you are as a designer."

Inspiration from Real Designers and Design Communities

Learning from others is a powerful way to discover your own voice. Here are a few ways to get inspired:

1.Follow Inspiring Designers:

•Look up designers who inspire you. Study their portfolios and think about what makes their work unique.

Example: Jessica Walsh, known for her bold and colorful designs, or Stefan Sagmeister, who blends art with storytelling.

2.Join Design Communities:

•Online platforms like Behance, Dribbble, and Instagram are full of talented designers sharing their work.

•Bonus: Many communities host challenges that can help you step out of your comfort zone.

3.Attend Events and Workshops:

•Whether it's an online webinar or a local design meetup, connecting with others can spark fresh ideas.

4.Explore Other Art Forms:

•Creativity isn't limited to design. Visit art galleries, watch films, or listen to music to find unexpected sources of inspiration.

Case Study:

A young designer, Mia, struggled to find her style until she joined an online design challenge on Instagram. Each prompt pushed her to explore different techniques. Over time, she noticed a recurring theme in her work—she loved creating bold, typographic posters with vibrant colors. Today, Mia runs her own studio specializing in poster design.

Fun Fact:

"Paula Scher, one of the most celebrated designers, often says her best ideas come from playful experiments rather than strict planning."

How Humor and Lightness Can Help Your Style

Design can feel overwhelming, especially when trying to find your voice. Adding a touch of humor and lightness can make the process enjoyable:

1.Laugh at Your Early Work:

•Look back at your first designs and appreciate how far you've come.

•"Remember, even the most talented designers started with awkward sketches!"

2.Don't Take It Too Seriously:

•Experiment with funny concepts or unexpected elements. Sometimes, playfulness leads to brilliance.

3.Incorporate Fun Elements:

•Create designs inspired by silly ideas, like a logo for an imaginary superhero or a pattern based on your favorite snack.

Pro Tip:

"Your style should bring you joy. If it feels like a chore, you're probably trying too hard."

Practical Exercise: Create a Design That Reflects Your Personality

This exercise is all about exploring who you are as a designer.

Objective:

Create a simple design (e.g., a poster, logo, or illustration) that reflects your personality, values, and style.

Steps:

1.Choose Your Theme:

•Think about what defines you—your hobbies, values, or favorite memories.

2.Pick Your Colors and Fonts:

•Use colors and fonts that resonate with your mood and personality.

Example: Bright, playful colors for an extroverted personality or muted tones for a calm and introspective vibe.

3.Incorporate Personal Elements:

•Add symbols or patterns that hold personal meaning to you.

4.Create Your Design:

•Sketch out your idea, then bring it to life using digital tools.

5.Share Your Work:

•Post your design in an online community or show it to friends. Ask for feedback to refine your style further.

Motivational Note:

"This exercise isn't about perfection—it's about self-expression. Let your design tell your story."

Key Takeaways

•Your creative voice is a blend of your experiences, influences, and personal style.

•Mistakes and experiments are essential parts of the creative process.

•Humor and lightness can make the journey of finding your style enjoyable.

•Design communities and challenges are excellent resources for growth and inspiration.

•Creating designs that reflect your personality is a powerful way to build your confidence as a designer.

Звісно, давайте розширимо попередній великий розділ і додамо всі необхідні вправи та приклади для досягнення більших обсягів. Ось розширений варіант з додатковими елементами:

4. The Business of Graphic Design: Freelancing or Agency Work?

The field of graphic design offers two major career paths: freelancing and working in an agency. Both have their unique benefits and challenges, and the choice between them depends on your goals, work style, and personal preferences. This section will provide a deeper understanding of both options, offering insights into what each path involves and how you can decide which one is right for you.

Chapter 11

Creating a Brand Identity

What is Brand Identity?

Brand identity is the collection of visual and non-visual elements that help a brand establish a unique presence in the market. It encompasses everything from the logo, typography, color palette, and imagery to the overall tone and voice of the brand. A strong brand identity builds recognition, trust, and emotional connection with your audience.

A brand identity is more than just a logo—it's the story that communicates a brand's mission, values, and what it stands for. It differentiates your brand from others, helps customers identify with your products, and ensures consistency across various marketing channels.

Real-Life Case Study: Apple

Apple's brand identity is globally recognized for its clean, minimalist design and sleek user experience. From its iconic logo to the packaging and advertising, Apple maintains a consistent message of innovation, elegance, and simplicity. The company's visual identity plays a massive role in shaping the perception of its products as premium, cutting-edge, and user-friendly.

Key Elements of Brand Identity

1.Logo Design

•The logo is often the first thing people associate with your brand. It must reflect the brand's personality, values, and what it represents. A great logo is simple, timeless, and versatile. It should be recognizable in both large and small formats and should communicate your brand's core message at a glance.

Example: The Nike "Swoosh" is a perfect example of a successful logo. Simple, dynamic, and instantly recognizable, it conveys motion, speed, and athleticism—core values of Nike.

2.Color Palette

•Colors play a vital role in shaping consumer perceptions. Different colors evoke different emotions and can influence buying behavior. A well-chosen color palette should be consistent across all branding materials to establish brand recognition.

Example: Coca-Cola uses red and white to convey excitement, energy, and refreshment, while Tiffany & Co. uses a signature shade of blue, known as "Tiffany Blue," to evoke luxury, elegance, and exclusivity.

3.Typography

•Typography refers to the selection and arrangement of fonts that complement your brand identity. The fonts you choose should align with your brand's voice—whether that's modern, traditional, playful, or sophisticated. Fonts are a powerful tool to establish consistency across your design elements.

Example: Google's clean, sans-serif fonts convey a sense of modernity, accessibility, and simplicity, while Chanel's elegant serif fonts are used to signify luxury, tradition, and timeless beauty.

4.Visual Style and Imagery

•The way your brand uses images, patterns, graphics, and layouts plays a key role in communicating its message. Visual style should be consistent and reflect the brand's tone and values. Whether using photography or illustration, the images you choose should resonate with your target audience.

Example: Starbucks employs a warm, earthy color palette and images of coffee beans and nature to convey a sense of comfort and relaxation, aligning with its brand promise of creating a "third place" between home and work.

How to Create a Brand Identity

1.Understand the Brand's Mission and Values

•Before you begin designing any visual elements, you need to fully understand what the brand stands for. Ask your client questions such as: What problem does the brand solve? What makes the brand unique? What emotions do you want the brand to evoke in people? This will guide every design choice you make.

2.Research the Target Audience

•Creating an effective brand identity starts with understanding the audience it's meant to reach. Research who they are, what they care about, and how they perceive the world. This allows you to design something that resonates with them and speaks to their values.

•Psychographics: In addition to basic demographics, you should also understand your audience's lifestyle, attitudes, and beliefs. This will help you tailor the brand identity to emotionally connect with them.

Example: A fitness brand aimed at millennials would likely focus on bold, energetic colors and dynamic, active imagery, whereas a luxury brand would use muted tones and sophisticated visuals.

3.Brainstorm and Sketch Ideas

•Once you understand the brand and its audience, it's time to brainstorm ideas. Use mind mapping, sketching, and mood boards to explore different concepts. Experiment with various shapes, symbols, and layouts to find something that visually communicates the brand's core message.

4.Refine and Test

•Once you have a few solid concepts, start refining them. Test different combinations of colors, typography, and logo designs. Create mockups to visualize how the brand identity will appear across various platforms, such as a website, business cards, social media, and packaging.

Practical Exercise: Create a brand identity for a fictional company specializing in eco-friendly products. Start by developing a logo, selecting a color palette, and choosing fonts. Then, create mockups of how the brand identity would look on a website homepage and product labels.

How to Maintain Consistency in Your Brand Identity

Once you've developed a brand identity, it's essential to maintain consistency across all platforms and materials. Consistency builds brand recognition and trust. Here are a few tips:

1.Create a Brand Guidelines Document

•A brand guidelines document ensures that everyone who works on the brand follows the same rules. It should include instructions on how to use the logo, color palette, typography, imagery, and other visual elements. This document is a reference to maintain consistency.

2.Review and Update Regularly

•As the brand grows and evolves, its identity may need updating. However, any updates should maintain the core essence of the brand. Consistency is key, but so is adapting to changes in the market or technology.

Example: Pepsi has updated its logo and branding over the years, but the core elements—bold red, blue, and white colors—have remained consistent, reinforcing the brand's identity over time.

Case Studies of Brand Identity Evolution

Many successful brands have evolved their identities to adapt to changing times. Understanding this process can help you make smarter decisions when developing your own brand identity.

•McDonald's: The brand's logo has evolved from a simple, retro design to the iconic golden arches. Their visual identity has remained consistent across decades, helping them retain worldwide recognition.

•Gap: In 2010, Gap unveiled a new logo, which led to an immediate backlash. After just one week of negative feedback, they reverted to the original logo, reinforcing the importance of listening to consumer feedback and being aware of public perception.

Conclusion: **Why Brand Identity Matters**

A brand identity is far more than just a logo. It's the visual representation of a brand's values, mission, and connection with its audience. A well-thought-out brand identity can build recognition, foster loyalty, and make your brand memorable. As a designer, mastering the creation of strong brand identities will be one of the most valuable skills in your career.

Practical Exercise:

Revisit the brand identity you created for your fictional company and assess how well it aligns with the company's mission and values. Adjust the design where necessary to better reflect the target audience's preferences and expectations.

This expanded chapter provides a deeper dive into the process of creating a brand identity. It covers everything from the core elements of a brand's visual identity to real-world examples of successful branding strategies. It also includes practical exercises to help you develop your own brand identity and start applying these skills in your design work.

Chapter 12

Working with Clients: From Brief to Design

What to do when working with clients?

As a beginner graphic designer, you will often face the challenge of working with clients. Understanding how to work with clients is a crucial part of your career. Clients come to you with specific requests, and your job is to create a design that meets their needs while maintaining your creative integrity.

The first step in working with a client is to obtain a clear brief. A brief is the foundation of your work. It outlines what needs to be created, what the design's goal is, any constraints or requirements, and what the client's expectations are. If the brief is unclear or vague, it may lead to misunderstandings and unnecessary revisions down the road.

How to get the right brief?

To obtain a good brief, it's essential to ask the right questions. Here are some key questions that will help you understand your client's needs:

Key Questions for the Brief:

•What exactly do you need created? Is it a logo, poster, website, or another design element?

•What is the goal of this project? Is the purpose to advertise, brand, or something else?

•Who is the target audience? Is it young people, adults, professionals, etc.?

•Do you have any specific colors, fonts, or styles you prefer? This will help you understand the aesthetic style your client is after.

•Are there any examples of designs you like? This gives you a clearer understanding of what the client envisions.

•What technical requirements are there? For instance, do you need different formats for print and web?

These questions will help you clarify what the client wants, ensuring that you don't waste time and effort on a design that doesn't meet their needs.

Practical Exercise: Create a brief for a fictional client who needs a logo for an eco-product startup. Consider all aspects: target audience, style, color scheme, and fonts.

The Process of Working with Clients

Once you receive a clear brief, the next step is to begin developing the design concept. This stage often involves creating initial drafts or mockups for review. Let's look at a famous example of the Nike logo.

Case Study: Nike – Logo Development

The Nike logo, known as the "Swoosh," was designed to symbolize movement and speed. Designer Carolyn Davidson created the logo with simplicity and elegance, reflecting the concept of athletic achievement. Her design was simple, but effective — it used just a symbol, without any text.

How to apply this in your practice?

After receiving the brief, you can create a few concept options for your client. For example, you could use simple geometric shapes that symbolize nature and incorporate earthy colors.

Feedback and Revisions

One of the most critical stages is feedback from the client. Clients may have specific requests or suggestions that you need to incorporate into the design. It's important not to take criticism personally. Client feedback helps improve and refine your work.

Case Study: Airbnb – Feedback Process

When Airbnb updated its logo in 2014, they received a lot of feedback indicating the logo was too complex and not intuitive. The logo was simplified to make it more universally appealing, and the design was adjusted based on this feedback.

How can you use this approach?

Once you receive feedback, review it with an open mind. Apply the suggestions that make sense, and don't be afraid to make major revisions if necessary. Always ask for clarification if something isn't clear.

Finalizing the Design

Once the client approves the concept and provides feedback, it's time to finalize the design. This involves preparing all necessary files in the required formats, such as AI, EPS, PNG, and PDF, for different uses (web and print).

Case Study: Dropbox – Finalizing the Design

Dropbox, another example of brand evolution, refined its logo over time based on client feedback and a growing need for simplicity. The company chose a cleaner, more modern design that worked well across digital platforms and marketing materials.

How to apply this in your work?

When you've got final approval from the client, make sure to prepare files for various formats, whether it's for digital media or print. Ensure each file is high resolution and ready for the platform it's meant for.

How to Work with Client Requests Without Losing Creativity

Sometimes, clients may request changes that contradict your creative vision. It can be difficult, but it's important to stay balanced.

Case Study: Coca-Cola – Balancing Creativity and Client Requests

Coca-Cola's logo is a prime example of how a company maintained its originality while adapting the design to modern trends. Even as the logo evolved, Coca-Cola kept the original elements, like the distinctive script, while updating its style.

How can you apply this in your work?

When clients ask for changes, it's important to explain why certain elements work and how they will benefit the project. However, don't be afraid to offer alternatives that still allow you to maintain the essence of the design.

Working with Multiple Clients at Once

If you're working as a freelancer or in an agency, you'll often need to handle several clients simultaneously. It's important to develop time management skills to stay organized and on track.

Case Study: Freelance Designer – Managing Multiple Projects

A freelance designer often has to balance various projects for different clients. Using project management tools like Trello or Asana can help you stay on top of tasks and deadlines for each project.

Practical Tip: Use a tool like Trello to track all your ongoing projects. Break each project into smaller tasks and set deadlines for each phase. This will help you manage multiple clients without feeling overwhelmed.

The Psychology of Client Work

Working with clients also involves managing expectations and dealing with difficult situations. Sometimes clients may not understand design concepts or may request excessive revisions. It's essential to be prepared to handle these situations with professionalism.

Case Study: Handling Difficult Clients

One famous example of working with a demanding client is Apple. Steve Jobs was notorious for his exacting standards and high expectations from designers. He would frequently ask designers to start over if the result didn't match his vision. However, Jobs' involvement resulted in some of the most iconic designs in the tech world, like the Apple logo and the design of the first iPhone.

How to apply this in your work?

Learn how to manage client expectations from the beginning by setting clear boundaries and being transparent about what is achievable within the project's budget and timeline.

Practical Exercise

Create a brief for a fictional client, define the project goals, the target audience, and design preferences. After that, create a few initial design concepts and request feedback from your friends or colleagues. Apply the feedback you receive and refine the designs.

Summary

Working with clients is a crucial skill for any graphic designer. By effectively communicating with clients, managing feedback, and maintaining creativity while respecting client requests, you will be able to produce designs that meet both creative and business goals. Learning to navigate this relationship is key to building a successful career in graphic design.

Chapter 13

Mastering Design Feedback

Feedback is an essential part of the design process. As a designer, you need to learn how to both receive and give feedback constructively. Whether you're working as a freelancer, in an agency, or in a team, how you handle feedback will significantly impact your design skills and the success of your projects. In this section, we'll dive into how to approach feedback in a way that helps you grow as a designer.

How to Receive and Process Feedback

One of the most important skills to develop as a designer is learning to receive feedback without taking it personally. The ability to listen to criticism and use it to improve your design is essential for long-term growth.

Step 1: Listen Without Interrupting

When a client or colleague provides feedback, listen attentively. Let them explain their thoughts fully before reacting. This not only shows respect but helps you understand their perspective clearly. Often, what's said might sound harsh at first, but when you step back and listen, it may reveal critical insights.

Example:

•Imagine working on a logo for a fashion brand. The client says, "I'm not feeling the modern, minimalist vibe you've gone for." Instead of defensively justifying your design, ask for clarification: "Could you tell me more about how you envision the brand identity?" This allows the client to provide more insight into their vision.

Step 2: Don't Take It Personally

Design feedback is about improving the work, not a reflection of your skills or personal worth. As a designer, it's essential to separate yourself from the work, which allows you to process feedback objectively.

Example:

•David Carson, a famous graphic designer, recalls instances when clients didn't like his unconventional typography. Instead of taking offense, he worked with the client's preferences while keeping his unique style intact, which resulted in a much stronger design.

Step 3: Clarify

If the feedback isn't clear, ask for specific examples. It's important to understand the exact issue. Ask questions like, "Can you point out which part of the design feels off to you?" or "What message do you want the design to convey more strongly?"

Example:

•A client might say, "This design feels too busy." Instead of assuming they mean your layout is cluttered, ask, "Are you referring to the amount of text, the color palette, or the overall structure of the layout?"

Step 4: Use the Feedback Constructively

After receiving feedback, reflect on it critically. Does the feedback help you see the design from a different perspective? Can you improve the design by making changes based on the feedback? Always aim to grow and improve, and view feedback as a way to develop your design skills.

Practical Exercise:

•Ask a fellow designer to review your work at various stages. Get feedback on specific design choices like typography, composition, and color theory. Reflect on their comments and implement the changes they suggest.

Real-Life Case Studies: Successful and Not-So-Successful Feedback

Real-Life Case Study 1:

Overcoming Creative Differences

•Company: A design agency working with a high-end fashion brand.

•Challenge: The client wanted a complete redesign of their visual identity, but the designer believed the current look was strong and iconic.

•Outcome: After receiving feedback, the designer carefully listened to the client's vision and worked collaboratively to incorporate elements that aligned with the client's aesthetic while maintaining the integrity of the brand's identity. The result was a more refined, yet fresh design that satisfied both parties.

•Key Takeaway: Effective communication and willingness to compromise can lead to a more polished and fitting outcome.

Real-Life Case Study 2:

The Power of Constructive Feedback

•Freelancer: A freelance designer working on a website redesign for a tech startup.

•Challenge: The client was dissatisfied with the homepage because it lacked the bold, innovative feel they wanted.

•Outcome: Rather than taking it personally, the designer discussed the feedback with the client and refined the typography, layout, and color scheme to better reflect the brand's tone. The final design exceeded the client's expectations and was well-received.

•Key Takeaway: Constructive feedback provides direction, helping designers hone in on exactly what needs improvement and how to achieve the desired result.

How to Handle Negative or Conflicting Feedback

Sometimes, feedback can feel contradictory, especially when different stakeholders provide different opinions. How do you handle conflicting feedback?

Example:

•Imagine receiving feedback from two clients: one wants a minimalist design, while the other wants something more intricate and bold. In this case, prioritize the business goals and try to merge both approaches. Present a design that aligns with the client's broader objectives, while finding a middle ground that addresses both opinions.

Practical Tip:

If you receive conflicting feedback, ask clarifying questions and ensure everyone involved is on the same page about the end goal of the design. Suggest possible compromises that still stay true to the project's goals.

The Importance of Continuous Learning and Adapting to Feedback

Feedback is a powerful tool not only for improving a single design but for advancing your overall skill set. By listening to feedback regularly and integrating it into your process, you'll improve over time.

Example:

•As you progress in your design career, you might notice patterns in the feedback you receive. Perhaps clients frequently point out that your typography is too complex or that your color choices are too bold. Recognizing these trends will help you refine these skills over time.

Practical Tip:

Create a feedback journal where you track recurring issues and improvement areas. Over time, you'll see the areas where you need to focus your learning and development.

Feedback Loops and Client Communication

It's essential to build effective feedback loops with your clients to ensure you're on the right track throughout the project. Feedback shouldn't be left until the very end—it should be part of the process.

Example:

•For each milestone, such as the first design draft or a wireframe, request feedback before continuing. This helps prevent you from investing too much time on a design that might not align with the client's expectations.

Practical Tip:

Set up regular check-ins with your client to review progress and gather feedback. This proactive approach reduces the risk of costly revisions later on.

Creating a Positive Feedback Culture

If you're working in a team or agency, it's vital to establish a positive feedback culture. This means fostering an environment where feedback is seen as an opportunity for growth rather than a critique.

Example:

•In creative studios like Pentagram or Frog Design, feedback is an integral part of the process. Designers are encouraged to share their ideas, offer suggestions, and listen to feedback from other team members. This culture leads to more refined designs and a collaborative atmosphere.

Practical Tip:

Encourage open communication and respect for different opinions within your team. When feedback is shared in a constructive and supportive environment, it drives creativity and fosters growth for everyone involved.

Conclusion: **Mastering Feedback for Design Growth**

Mastering feedback is not just about receiving or giving critiques—it's about understanding that feedback is an essential part of growing as a designer. Whether you're freelancing or working in an agency, learning to handle feedback, using it to your advantage, and integrating it into your process will make you a more effective and successful designer.

Additional Tips:

•Embrace feedback as a tool for growth. It will help you become more adaptable, creative, and skilled as a designer.

•Keep your portfolio up to date based on feedback to showcase the best of your evolving work.

•Always ask for feedback. The best designers constantly seek input to refine their work and skills.

Chapter 14

The Business of Graphic Design: Freelancing or Agency Work?

The first decision you need to make as a graphic designer is whether to pursue freelancing or to work in a design agency. Each career path offers a distinct work environment, client base, and daily experience.

•Freelancing gives you the freedom to work on a variety of projects for different clients, set your own hours, and work from anywhere. However, it also requires you to handle the business side of things—marketing, managing clients, negotiating contracts, and more.

•Agency Work, on the other hand, provides structure, a steady income, and the opportunity to work within a creative team. Agencies usually have multiple designers with complementary skills, allowing for collaboration on large-scale projects. However, you may have less creative freedom and more restrictions, and agency work can often involve long hours and tight deadlines.

Example:

•Freelancing: Take Jessica Walsh, a prominent designer known for her freelance work and creative projects. She transitioned from agency life to build her own business and creative studio, where she takes on diverse projects from clients all around the world.

•Agency Work: Pentagram, one of the world's most famous design agencies, offers its designers the opportunity to collaborate with a global team, working on high-profile projects for clients like Mastercard, Microsoft, and the Guggenheim.

The Freelance Life: Finding Clients, Contracts, and Pricing Your Work

Freelancing can be incredibly rewarding if you thrive on independence and flexibility, but it also comes with the challenge of building a client base and managing business operations.

•Finding Clients:

•Networking: Attend industry events, webinars, or online communities to connect with potential clients. Networking is one of the most effective ways to grow your freelance business.

•Portfolio Websites: Having a strong online presence with a professional portfolio website is essential. Platforms like Behance, Dribbble, and Adobe Portfolio can help you showcase your work to attract clients.

•Cold Outreach: Don't be afraid to reach out directly to companies or individuals whose work aligns with your skills. Send an introductory email with a link to your portfolio and a clear pitch.

•Contracts:

It's crucial to have a contract for every project, even if you have a personal relationship with the client. Contracts protect both parties and ensure clear expectations on deliverables, payment, and deadlines. A good contract should include:

•Scope of work

•Payment terms

•Deadlines and milestones

•Revisions and approval processes

•Pricing Your Work:

Setting the right price for your services can be tricky, especially when starting out. Consider the following:

•Hourly Rate: Ideal for shorter or more open-ended projects. Research the average rates in your area or industry to set competitive prices.

•Project-Based Pricing: For larger projects, charge a fixed rate based on the scope of work.

•Value-Based Pricing: Charge according to the value your design provides to the client, especially for high-impact projects such as branding.

Example:

•Freelancer: Chris Do, the founder of The Futur, runs a successful design consultancy while offering advice on pricing, contracts, and client management to other freelancers through his YouTube channel and online courses.

How to Work in an Agency: Benefits and Drawbacks

Working in a design agency offers a structured environment, but it comes with its own set of pros and cons.

•Benefits of Working in an Agency:

•Collaboration: Agencies provide a collaborative environment, where you can work alongside other designers, copywriters, developers, and marketing specialists. This allows for a more integrated approach to design and the opportunity to learn from others.

•Steady Workflow: Agencies typically have a constant flow of clients and projects, offering financial stability and fewer uncertainties about workload.

•Mentorship and Growth: You'll likely have access to senior designers or managers who can mentor you and help you grow in your craft.

•Drawbacks of Working in an Agency:

•Less Creative Freedom: Agency work often requires you to follow the client's vision and guidelines, which might limit your creative freedom.

•Longer Hours: Agency deadlines can be tight, and you might need to work long hours to meet client expectations.

•Team Dynamics: While working in a team is a benefit for collaboration, it can sometimes be challenging when balancing differing creative opinions and personalities.

Example:

•Agency Work: At Frog Design, designers collaborate on large-scale projects with global clients. While the projects can be high-profile, designers often work under strict timelines and must align with the agency's vision.

*Practical Exercise: B*uilding Your Professional Portfolio and Client Acquisition Strategy

Creating a solid portfolio is one of the most important steps in building your career, whether you are freelancing or working in an agency.

Step 1: Build Your Portfolio

•Select your best work that showcases your strengths as a designer. Include diverse projects that reflect your versatility.

•Ensure your portfolio is easy to navigate, with high-quality images and brief descriptions of each project.

Step 2: Client Acquisition Strategy

•Define your ideal client. Who do you want to work with? What kind of projects excite you?

•Create a targeted outreach strategy. Start with personal connections and build from there by reaching out to potential clients through email or social media.

•Set a pricing structure that aligns with your experience and the value you provide.

Example:

•Freelancer Portfolio: A good example of a strong freelance portfolio is Robby Leonardi, a freelance designer whose portfolio showcases interactive design projects with great detail. Robby not only presents his design work but also includes case studies that explain the process behind each project.

The Psychology of Client Work

Understanding the psychology behind client work is crucial to building long-term relationships and delivering projects that align with their vision.

•Managing Client Expectations: Clients often have high expectations and a vision, but they may not fully understand the design process. It's important to educate your client on the process, the time it takes, and what you can and cannot do.

•Handling Difficult Clients: Sometimes, clients will change their minds midway through a project, which can be frustrating. Learning how to handle these situations with patience and professionalism is key.

•Understanding Feedback: Clients may not always give constructive feedback. It's important to ask specific questions to guide them in providing useful insights.

Example:

•Difficult Clients: Olafur Eliasson, a famous artist and designer, shares how he had to deal with conflicting opinions and adjust his work accordingly to please multiple stakeholders in a large collaborative project.

Time Management and Working with Deadlines

Another important aspect of working with clients, whether as a freelancer or in an agency, is managing your time and meeting deadlines.

•Time-Tracking Tools: Use tools like Toggl or Harvest to track your working hours and manage multiple projects efficiently.

•Setting Realistic Deadlines: Make sure to factor in time for revisions, feedback, and unexpected issues when setting deadlines.

•Prioritizing Tasks: Prioritize your tasks based on their importance and the client's needs. Break large projects into smaller, manageable tasks to ensure timely completion.

Conclusion: **Navigating Your Graphic Design Career**

Choosing between freelancing and agency work in graphic design depends on your personal goals and preferences. Freelancing provides flexibility and independence but requires self-management and business savvy, while agency work offers stability but can limit your creative freedom. Building a strong portfolio, networking, and understanding client relations will help you succeed in either path.

No matter which path you choose, remember to keep learning, refining your skills, and developing relationships with clients and colleagues. Your future as a graphic designer is shaped by the choices you make today, and whether you decide to freelance or work in an agency, your journey is just beginning.

Practical Tips for Success:

•Never underestimate the power of networking and building a solid online presence.

•Focus on building a portfolio that demonstrates your ability to solve real-world design problems.

•Whether freelancing or working in an agency, always keep learning and stay up to date with the latest design trends and tools.

Chapter 15

Digital vs. Print Design: Understanding the Difference

Design is a vast and multifaceted field, and one of the key distinctions every designer must understand is the difference between digital and print design. While both share fundamental design principles, the techniques, tools, and requirements for each can differ significantly. This section will explore these differences and provide actionable advice on how to approach both forms of design.

Digital vs. Print Design: Key Differences

At the core, the distinction between digital and print design is largely technical, but it also affects the way designs are created, executed, and delivered.

•Digital Design is intended to be viewed on screens—whether on smartphones, laptops, tablets, or desktops. This design style must adapt to various screen sizes, resolutions, and even user interfaces. It is dynamic, meaning the design may change in response to user interaction, such as buttons being clicked or images being zoomed in on.

•Print Design, on the other hand, is static. Once a design is printed, it remains the same. Print design involves creating designs for physical mediums like posters, brochures, packaging, and business cards. The designer must consider paper texture, color reproduction, and physical layout dimensions, as well as how the piece will be printed (e.g., offset printing or digital printing).

Key Differences:

•Color: Digital design uses RGB (Red, Green, Blue) color model, while print design uses CMYK (Cyan, Magenta, Yellow, and Black). This difference affects the way colors are displayed on screens versus on paper.

•Resolution: Digital designs are typically created at a lower resolution, usually 72 DPI (dots per inch), as screens do not require as much detail. In contrast, print designs require a much higher resolution (300 DPI) to ensure the design appears sharp and clear on paper.

•Size and Format: Digital designs need to be flexible, responsive, and optimized for a variety of screen sizes. Print designs, however, have specific sizes that are dictated by paper dimensions and printing requirements.

Preparing Files for Print: What You Need to Know

When transitioning from digital to print, one of the most important aspects to keep in mind is file preparation. Print files need to be set up in a specific way to ensure high-quality output.

1. Resolution Matters

Unlike digital designs that are created at 72 DPI, print designs must be created at 300 DPI to ensure that the image appears crisp when printed. Low-resolution files (under 150 DPI) will look pixelated and unprofessional in print.

2. Color Mode

Switch your color mode from RGB to CMYK when preparing files for print. RGB is designed for screens and light-based color, while CMYK is designed for pigment-based color used in printing. Using the right color mode ensures the final print colors match what you see on your screen as closely as possible.

3. Bleed and Margins

A bleed refers to the area outside of the document's trim lines that will be trimmed off after printing. It ensures that there are no white edges where the design may have been misaligned. Typically, a 0.125-inch bleed is recommended for most designs. Make sure all critical text and logos stay within the margins, as anything too close to the edges may be cut off.

4. File Types

For print, use file formats like PDF, TIFF, or EPS to ensure the highest quality. These file types preserve resolution and allow for more complex color management. Avoid file types like JPEG, as they may compress the image and reduce quality.

How Brands Adapt Designs for Digital and Print Platforms

Many successful brands understand the importance of adapting their designs for both digital and print platforms. Let's take a look at some interesting examples:

•Mailchimp:

Mailchimp, an email marketing service, exemplifies how to adapt design across digital and print. Their digital campaigns often feature bright colors, animation, and interactive elements to capture attention. In contrast, their print ads rely on simplicity, clean typography, and clear imagery to communicate the brand's straightforwardness.

Key Takeaway:

Mailchimp shows how important it is to adjust the design's style and tone depending on the platform. Digital designs should be dynamic and engaging, while print materials should be clean and easy to read.

•Glossier:

Glossier, a popular cosmetics brand, effectively adapts their design for both digital and print. Their digital content is minimalistic with strong emphasis on product images and white space.

In print materials like brochures and product packaging, Glossier adds textures and more intimate visual elements to connect with the consumer on a deeper level.

Key Takeaway:

Glossier highlights how design elements like color, texture, and photography can be adjusted to fit the medium. Digital channels emphasize engagement, while print materials focus on emotional connection and product experience.

•Everlane:

Everlane, a fashion brand, keeps their designs consistent across platforms but adapts them to fit the medium. Their digital designs focus on simplicity and accessibility, with clean lines and intuitive navigation. On the other hand, their print materials, such as catalogs and packaging, emphasize the high-quality photography of their products.

Key Takeaway:

Everlane demonstrates how adapting design to the medium, while staying true to the brand, is essential. Digital spaces prioritize clarity and ease, while print materials highlight the quality of the product itself.

•Patagonia:

Patagonia, an outdoor clothing brand, uses impactful imagery of nature in their digital campaigns. Their website and social media posts feature high-energy visuals that convey their eco-friendly message. However, in print materials like brochures or product packaging, the focus shifts to environmental sustainability, using raw, nature-inspired designs that align with their brand's core values.

Key Takeaway:

Patagonia shows how aligning the message of the brand with its design across all platforms enhances the overall customer experience. Digital and print designs serve different purposes but are both integral to conveying the brand's ethos.

•Warby Parker:

Warby Parker, a trendy eyewear brand, integrates a clean and cohesive design across both their digital and print platforms. While their website and ads are bright, engaging, and interactive, their print materials, like eyewear catalogs and flyers, focus more on minimalist, straightforward designs that prioritize readability and elegance.

Key Takeaway:

Warby Parker demonstrates how to adapt a consistent visual identity for different channels. While digital designs use bold, engaging visuals, print materials focus on simplicity and elegance to ensure the product is the star.

Practical Exercise: Create a Poster for Print and Adapt It for Social Media

Now that you understand the basics of digital and print design, let's dive into a practical exercise.

1.Create a Poster for Print:

Start by designing a poster for an upcoming event, product, or campaign. Make sure to use the proper dimensions and include a 0.125-inch bleed. Focus on using CMYK colors and a high resolution (300 DPI).

2.Adapt the Poster for Social Media:

Once your poster is complete, adapt it for use on social media platforms. Consider the dimensions for Instagram posts, Facebook covers, and Twitter banners. Since digital designs need to be optimized for various devices, ensure the design looks good both on mobile and desktop screens. Adjust the color palette, typography, and size to ensure it works effectively for each platform.

Conclusion: The Digital-Print Design Journey

Understanding the differences between digital and print design is essential for any designer looking to make their mark in the field. Each medium requires different technical approaches, but both share the same design principles: clarity, simplicity, and strong visual communication.

Whether you're creating a website, an app, or a printed flyer, learning how to adapt your design to its final medium will set you up for success. Remember to always check your files for resolution, color mode, and format before finalizing them for either digital or print. By mastering these aspects, you'll be able to create designs that look professional and polished across all platforms.

Chapter 16

Moving Forward: Your Next Steps

You've reached the final chapter of this guide. By now, you've learned the basics of graphic design, explored different tools and techniques, and even created your first designs. But this is just the beginning of your journey.

In this chapter, we'll discuss how to evaluate your progress, build a portfolio that showcases your work, and continue learning to grow as a designer. Let's take the next steps together.

How to Evaluate Your Progress

Tracking your growth as a designer is essential for staying motivated and improving your skills. Here's how to do it effectively:

1.Reflect on Your Work:

•Look back at your earliest designs and compare them to your recent ones.

•Notice areas where you've improved, such as composition, color use, or typography.

2.Seek Constructive Feedback:

•Share your work with trusted friends, mentors, or online communities.

•Ask specific questions like, "Does this design communicate the intended message?" or "What could make this more effective?"

3.Set Milestones:

•Break your goals into achievable steps.

Example: "In the next three months, I'll create a portfolio with five completed projects."

4.Embrace the Learning Process:

•Remember that design is a journey, not a destination. Every project teaches you something new.

Inspirational Note:

"Every expert was once a beginner who dared to try."

The Story of a Small Beginning

Mia, a young designer from a small town, started with nothing but a love for creativity and free software. She created fictional brands and posted her work on Behance. One day, her mockup for a vegan coffee shop caught the attention of a local business. That first project wasn't perfect, but it led to referrals, confidence, and a growing portfolio. Today, Mia runs her own studio, working with international clients.

Takeaway:

"Your journey doesn't need to start big—it just needs to start."

Building a Portfolio That Shines

A portfolio is your ticket to showcasing your skills and attracting opportunities. Here's how to create one that stands out:

1.Choose Your Best Work:

•Include 5-10 projects that highlight your strengths and versatility.

•Quality over quantity is key.

2.Showcase Diversity:

•Display a variety of designs, such as logos, social media posts, patterns, or illustrations.

•Tip: If you're just starting, create fictional projects to demonstrate your range.

3.Tell the Story Behind Your Designs:

•Explain the goals, challenges, and solutions for each project. This helps potential clients or employers understand your process.

4.Make It Visually Engaging:

•Use clean layouts and consistent typography. Treat your portfolio as a design project itself.

5.Host It Online:

•Use platforms like Behance, Dribbble, or even a personal website to share your portfolio.

Fun Fact:

"Did you know many designers got their first freelance jobs by showcasing fictional projects on Behance?"

Learning Never Stops

Graphic design is an ever-evolving field. Staying updated and connected is key to growing as a designer. Here's how to keep learning:

1.Online Courses:

•Skillshare, Coursera, Domestika—great platforms for skill-building.

2.Books to Inspire You:

•"Steal Like an Artist" by Austin Kleon: A guide to unlocking your creativity.

•"Thinking with Type" by Ellen Lupton: Perfect for mastering typography.

•"Logo Design Love" by David Airey: A practical guide to creating iconic logos.

3.Join Online Communities:

•Dribbble, Behance, Reddit (r/graphic_design).

Motivational Note:

"The best designers never stop learning. Every course, book, or conversation is a step forward."

Practical Exercise: Create Your Roadmap for Growth

Outline a roadmap for the next six months to a year, focusing on skills you want to improve and projects you want to complete.

Steps:

1.Set Specific Goals:

Example: "Learn how to create motion graphics" or "Redesign a website as a portfolio project."

2.Choose Resources:

•Find courses, books, or communities that align with your goals.

3.Plan Your Projects:

•Decide on the number and type of projects you want to include in your portfolio.

4.Schedule Regular Reviews:

•Set aside time every month to evaluate your progress and adjust your roadmap.

Your Final Step: Believe in Yourself

Design is not just about creating beautiful visuals—it's about solving problems, telling stories, and connecting with people. You've taken the first step by picking up this book and ¡exploring the world of design. Now, the next chapter is yours to write.

Motivational Note:

"You don't need to be perfect to start. You just need to start. Your journey, your voice, your designs—they all matter. Go out there and create something amazing."

The Future of Graphic Design: Trends and Innovations

Graphic design is a constantly evolving field. What was cutting-edge a few years ago may already feel outdated today. As technology advances, the landscape of design continues to shift, offering both new challenges and exciting opportunities for designers. This chapter will explore some of the most significant trends and innovations shaping the future of graphic design, and how you, as a designer, can stay ahead of the curve.

1. The Rise of Artificial Intelligence in Design

Artificial intelligence (AI) is no longer just a futuristic concept—it's already making waves in the design world. AI tools are transforming how we create and interact with designs, offering faster, more efficient ways to generate work and refine ideas.

How AI is Changing Design:

•AI-Powered Design Tools: Platforms like Canva and Adobe Sensei are incorporating AI to help automate tasks like resizing images, adjusting colors, and even suggesting design layouts. These tools can analyze trends and user preferences to generate personalized design templates, making it easier for designers to focus on creativity and strategy.

•Generative Design: AI algorithms can create multiple design variations based on initial input. By defining specific parameters, AI can suggest countless design solutions, allowing designers to explore a wider range of creative possibilities.

The Opportunity for Designers:

While AI can automate many tasks, it can never replace human creativity and intuition. Designers will still be needed to give a personal touch and refine the designs generated by AI. The key is learning how to use AI as a tool, rather than a replacement, to enhance your workflow and efficiency.

2. Virtual and Augmented Reality: A New Frontier for Design

Virtual reality (VR) and augmented reality (AR) are opening up entirely new avenues for graphic designers. As these technologies continue to evolve, they offer designers the opportunity to create immersive, interactive experiences that were once unimaginable.

The Role of Graphic Design in VR and AR:

•Immersive Experiences: VR and AR are being used to create interactive environments that allow users to experience design in a three-dimensional space. Designers will need to learn how to design not just for screens, but for environments that users can physically interact with, such as 360-degree websites, virtual stores, and interactive product demonstrations.

•Enhanced User Engagement: AR applications are already being used by brands like IKEA, which lets customers visualize furniture in their own homes through their smartphones. Designers are tasked with creating visually engaging experiences that integrate seamlessly with the real world.

The Opportunity for Designers:

As VR and AR technologies advance, designers will need to develop new skill sets, including understanding 3D space, motion graphics, and user experience in these new contexts. The demand for designers who can create engaging VR/AR content is expected to rise, so keeping an eye on these trends is essential for staying relevant.

3. Sustainability and Eco-friendly Design: A Growing Responsibility

With increasing awareness about environmental issues, more and more brands are prioritizing sustainability. Graphic designers are being called upon to create designs that not only meet aesthetic and functional goals but also align with environmentally friendly practices.

The Shift Toward Sustainability:

•Eco-conscious Materials and Printing: Designers are now asked to consider the environmental impact of their designs, from using recycled paper to choosing environmentally friendly inks. As sustainability becomes a key priority for brands, designers will need to balance aesthetic appeal with eco-conscious choices.

•Digital-First Design: Reducing waste is a major consideration. The shift towards digital products (websites, apps, etc.) helps minimize the use of physical materials, but designers must also consider how the digital experience can be more sustainable—such as reducing the carbon footprint of websites through efficient design.

The Opportunity for Designers:

As sustainability becomes a core value for companies and consumers, designers who embrace eco-friendly practices will be in high demand. From reducing paper waste to using digital solutions, designers will play a key role in creating a more sustainable future.

4. The Evolution of Typography: The Age of Variable Fonts

Typography has always been a crucial part of graphic design, and now, we are entering a new phase with variable fonts. These fonts allow designers to manipulate weight, width, slant, and other properties within a single font file, giving them more flexibility and control.

What Are Variable Fonts?

•More Flexibility: Variable fonts combine multiple styles of a typeface (like bold, italic, light, etc.) into one file, which allows designers to experiment with the look of the font on the fly. This reduces the need for multiple font files, making websites faster and more efficient.

•Improved User Experience: Variable fonts can adapt to different screen sizes and resolutions, providing a better user experience across devices.

The Opportunity for Designers:

Variable fonts give designers a unique opportunity to create dynamic, responsive typography that adjusts to the user's device and interaction. By mastering variable fonts, designers can improve the usability and aesthetics of their designs.

5. Data-Driven Design: Using Analytics to Drive Creativity

Data-driven design is an emerging trend where designers use user data, analytics, and research to inform their design decisions. This approach allows designers to make more informed choices, resulting in designs that are not only visually appealing but also more effective in achieving the goals of a project.

How Data Is Shaping Design:

•User-Centered Design: By analyzing user behavior, designers can create personalized experiences that better meet the needs of the target audience. For example, if analytics show that users are spending too much time looking for a certain feature, a designer can adjust the layout to make it more accessible.

•A/B Testing: Designers can now test different design options in real-time to see which one performs better. This iterative process ensures that the final design is optimized for its intended audience.

The Opportunity for Designers:

Data-driven design offers the opportunity to merge creativity with real-world performance. Designers who are comfortable working with data and analytics will be well-positioned to create designs that are not only beautiful but also highly effective in meeting user needs.

Conclusion: Embracing the Future of Design

The future of graphic design is exciting, fast-paced, and full of opportunities. By staying up-to-date with emerging trends like AI, AR/VR, sustainability, and data-driven design, you can ensure that your skills remain relevant and competitive. The key to thriving as a designer is adaptability—embracing new tools, technologies, and challenges will help you grow and evolve in this dynamic field.

As you continue on your design journey, remember that the most successful designers are those who not only master the tools of today but also anticipate the trends of tomorrow. Embrace innovation, keep learning, and most importantly, keep creating!

Designing with Purpose: Ethical Design and Social Responsibility

In today's world, design is no longer just about aesthetics; it's about making a meaningful impact. As designers, we are entrusted with the responsibility to create visual experiences that resonate not only with consumers but also with society at large. Ethical design is about understanding the social, cultural, and environmental implications of our creative choices. In this chapter, we'll explore how to integrate social responsibility and sustainability into your design work, while maintaining your creative voice.

1. The Role of Ethical Design in Graphic Design

Ethical design focuses on creating products, services, and campaigns that are respectful, inclusive, and responsible. Designers have a unique opportunity to shape perceptions, influence behavior, and advocate for positive change through their work. The choices you make—from colors and imagery to the materials you use—have the potential to contribute to a more sustainable and equitable world.

Why Ethical Design Matters:

•Impact on Society: Design isn't just visual; it influences behavior. Whether it's promoting positive health habits, raising awareness about social issues, or encouraging environmental responsibility, designers are in a position to shape the world around them.

•Consumer Expectations: Today's consumers are more aware than ever of the ethical practices of the brands they support. Brands that prioritize sustainability, inclusivity, and transparency tend to attract loyal, conscious consumers.

•Cultural Sensitivity: As global connectivity increases, designers must be aware of cultural nuances. What works in one region may not be effective—or may even be offensive—in another. Ethical design requires cultural understanding and sensitivity.

2. Sustainability in Design

One of the most pressing aspects of ethical design is sustainability. The environmental impact of design work has become a significant concern as industries continue to grow and evolve. Sustainability isn't just about using recycled materials or green technologies—it's about creating designs that leave a positive or minimal impact on the environment.

Ways to Integrate Sustainability into Your Design:

•Eco-Friendly Materials: When creating physical designs (like packaging, posters, or business cards), consider using materials that are recyclable, biodegradable, or made from sustainable sources.

•Digital Sustainability: Digital designs can also have an environmental impact. Optimizing your website design for speed and efficiency, using energy-efficient hosting, and reducing carbon footprints through minimalistic and efficient designs can make a difference.

•Product Lifecycle: Think about the entire lifecycle of your designs. Will they contribute to unnecessary waste? Can the designs be repurposed or reused? Sustainable design encourages rethinking how products and services can be used for a longer time.

Example:

•Patagonia, the clothing brand, has been a pioneer in promoting sustainability. Their packaging is minimalistic, their products are made from recycled materials, and they've implemented the "Worn Wear" initiative, which encourages customers to buy used products. Patagonia's design approach exemplifies how ethics and sustainability can work hand-in-hand.

3. Inclusivity and Accessibility in Design

Another key aspect of ethical design is ensuring that your designs are accessible to everyone, regardless of their background, abilities, or personal circumstances. Inclusive design is about removing barriers and ensuring that your work can be enjoyed and understood by the widest possible audience.

Inclusive Design Principles:

•Visual Accessibility: Ensure that text is legible, with high contrast between background and font color. Use accessible font sizes and types that can be easily read by those with visual impairments. Websites and apps should be navigable with screen readers and other assistive technologies.

•Cultural Sensitivity: Design in a way that respects cultural diversity. Avoid stereotypes and culturally inappropriate images or language. This shows respect for all audiences and prevents alienating potential customers.

•Universal Design: Universal design is about creating products and services that can be used by people of all abilities, regardless of age or disability. For instance, ensuring that your designs are responsive on different devices is part of this approach, as is making sure websites meet accessibility standards like WCAG (Web Content Accessibility Guidelines).

Example:

•Microsoft has done an excellent job of making its products accessible. They've incorporated accessibility tools into their design process, such as screen readers, keyboard navigation, and voice-activated controls. The company strives for inclusivity in every aspect of their digital designs.

4. The Power of Purpose-Driven Design

Purpose-driven design is about aligning your creative work with the values and mission of a brand or cause. It's about creating designs that aren't just beautiful but also have a positive impact on the world. Whether it's promoting social justice, advocating for the environment, or supporting education, your design can serve a greater purpose.

How to Design with Purpose:

•Aligning with a Cause: If you're working with a brand or organization, find out what values they stand for. Do they support environmental sustainability? Do they focus on diversity and inclusion? Aligning your design with these values will help the brand resonate more with its audience.

•Storytelling: Use design as a tool to tell stories that matter. Whether it's through visual narratives in advertisements, packaging, or digital media, storytelling can amplify the message of a brand or cause.

•Authenticity: Design with authenticity and transparency in mind. Consumers today are more likely to support brands that are open about their mission, the materials they use, and how their products are made.

Example:

•TOMS Shoes is a great example of purpose-driven design. The company's "One for One" campaign, where they donate a pair of shoes for every pair sold, was visually communicated through minimalist designs that highlighted their mission. Their design choices reinforced the message of social good.

5. Practical Exercise: Ethical Design for a Cause

Now it's your turn to apply what you've learned about ethical design. Choose a cause that matters to you—whether it's sustainability, social justice, or another cause—and create a visual design that communicates that cause. Here's how you can approach the exercise:

•Step 1: Research the cause and understand the values behind it. What message do you want to communicate through design?

•Step 2: Choose design elements that reflect the cause. This could be colors, imagery, or typography that convey the message.

•Step 3: Ensure your design is inclusive and accessible. Think about how it will resonate with a diverse audience.

•Step 4: Test your design. Show it to others and ask for feedback. Does it effectively communicate the cause? Is it visually accessible and inclusive?

Conclusion: Ethical Design Is the Future

As the design industry continues to evolve, ethical and purpose-driven design will only become more important. Designers have a unique responsibility to create work that not only looks good but also contributes to a better, more inclusive, and sustainable world. By embracing ethical design practices, you can help shape the future of the industry, one project at a time.

Remember, design has the power to change perceptions, influence behavior, and make a real-world impact. So, the next time you sit down to create, think about the bigger picture: How can your design contribute to a better world?

Conclusion: Embrace the Creative Adventure

Congratulations! You've just taken the first step into the exciting world of graphic design, and now the real adventure begins. You've learned the basics, discovered your tools, and started creating—but the journey doesn't end here. It's just the beginning of a lifelong learning process that will constantly challenge you and push you to grow as a designer.

Design is not about perfection, but about growth, learning, and pushing boundaries. Every mistake, every experiment, is an opportunity to refine your skills and strengthen your creative voice. There is no "perfect" design—there are only designs that communicate ideas, solve problems, and reflect who you are as a designer. The more you create, the more you'll discover about yourself, your style, and your craft.

Don't Be Afraid to Make Mistakes

Remember, design is not a straight line, and it certainly isn't about getting everything right from the start. The beauty of creativity lies in trial and error. You'll make mistakes—that's inevitable. The important thing is to learn from them and see them as part of the process. Each "failure" will teach you something valuable, helping you build resilience and adaptability. So embrace the missteps, the awkward phases, and the challenges. These moments will shape you into a stronger, more confident designer.

The Power of Experimentation

As you continue your journey, don't shy away from experimenting. Try new techniques, explore different styles, and push the limits of your comfort zone. Some of the most innovative and impactful designs have come from moments of trial, exploration, and creative risk-taking. It's in those moments of experimentation that you'll discover your true potential and find your unique creative voice.

Take time to test out new ideas, even if they seem unconventional or out of the ordinary. Remember, design is all about finding solutions and exploring new ways to communicate visually. So never be afraid to break the rules, challenge the status quo, and think outside the box. Sometimes, the best designs come from taking risks and experimenting with new approaches.

Stay Consistent and Keep Learning

The key to success in design, and in life, is persistence. The more you practice, the more confident and capable you'll become. But also remember that learning never stops. Design trends evolve, new tools and technologies emerge, and your own skills will continuously improve. So keep learning, stay curious, and always strive to improve. There is always more to learn, and the best designers are those who are open to growth and change.

Your Creativity Has Power

Your designs have the power to make a real difference. Whether you're designing for a brand, a cause, or a personal project, your work can inspire, inform, and connect people. Design isn't just about making beautiful things—it's about creating experiences that engage and resonate with others. Don't underestimate the impact your designs can have.

As you continue, remember that your designs have the potential to shape perceptions, change minds, and influence decisions. Whether it's creating designs for a non-profit, working with a client, or just experimenting with your own ideas, know that what you create matters. You have a unique perspective that the world needs, and your creativity is powerful.

Connecting with the Design Community

Design is not an isolated endeavor. It's a conversation—a dialogue between you, your clients, and the world. Your work will inspire others, just as you have been inspired by the work of those who came before you. Don't be afraid to share your designs, get feedback, and learn from the creative community around you. The more you connect with others, the more you'll grow as a designer. The design community is vast, supportive, and filled with talented people who are eager to share their knowledge and experiences. So don't be afraid to ask questions, offer help, and build meaningful relationships within this incredible community.

The Adventure Continues

The creative process is an adventure, and while it may feel overwhelming at times, it's all part of the journey. There will be days when you feel stuck or uninspired, and you may even question your abilities. But it's in these moments of challenge that you will learn the most. Remember, the most successful designers didn't get there by giving up during tough times—they pushed through the obstacles and emerged stronger on the other side.

You are not just designing; you are creating your future as a designer. Every project, every design you make, adds to your experience. You're building a portfolio, but more importantly, you're building your career, your confidence, and your unique perspective. Keep moving forward, and never stop creating.

Take the Next Step

Now, go ahead and put what you've learned into action. Create something today—whether it's a logo, a poster, a social media post, or just a simple sketch. It doesn't have to be perfect. The goal is to keep experimenting, pushing yourself, and enjoying the ride. Mistakes are part of the process, so don't be afraid of them. Every new creation is an opportunity to learn and grow.

The world is waiting for your creativity. The tools are in your hands, the knowledge is yours, and the possibilities are endless. Take that next step and see where your creative journey takes you. You're ready. Now, go ahead and create something amazing.

Acknowledgments

Writing this book has been an exciting and rewarding journey, and I owe my thanks to everyone who inspired me along the way.

To my mentors and the creative community—thank you for sharing your wisdom, your designs, and, most importantly, your mistakes. You've shown me that design isn't about perfection; it's about being brave enough to try, fail, and try again.

A special thanks to every beginner out there who has ever asked, "Where do I even start?" You inspired me to create this guide. This book is for you—the dreamers, the doers, and the "I-don't-know-what-I'm-doing-but-I'll-figure-it-out" adventurers. Remember, the only wrong step is not taking one.

And finally, to you, the reader—thank you for trusting me with your first steps into graphic design. Every masterpiece starts with a messy sketch, and every expert was once a beginner who refused to give up. So grab your tools, clear your space, and take the first step. The world is waiting for your creativity, and the adventure is just beginning.

Glossary

1.Alignment

The positioning of elements on a page, ensuring they are aligned along a common axis. Proper alignment helps create a sense of order and organization in a design.

2.Aspect Ratio

The proportional relationship between the width and height of an image or screen. For example, a 16:9 aspect ratio is commonly used in wide-screen displays.

3.Bleed

The area outside the trim line that ensures no white borders are visible after printing. It's essential in print design to extend images or backgrounds beyond the edges of the page.

4.CMYK (Cyan, Magenta, Yellow, Black)

A color model used in color printing, combining these four colors to produce a full spectrum of printed colors.

5.Contrast

The difference between light and dark areas in a design. High contrast helps make text or visuals stand out and enhances readability.

6.Curves (Bezier Curves)

A mathematical curve used in vector graphics that allows for precise manipulation of shapes and paths. Often used in Adobe Illustrator.

7.Typography

The art and technique of arranging type in design. This includes choosing fonts, setting type size, line spacing, and adjusting the spacing between characters (kerning).

8.Grid System

A framework of horizontal and vertical lines used to structure and organize content within a design. Grids help create consistency and alignment in layouts.

9.Hue

A color or shade, such as red, blue, or yellow, on the color wheel. It refers to the dominant wavelength of a color.

10.Kerning

The adjustment of space between two specific characters in a word. Proper kerning ensures that text is visually balanced.

11.Layers

Different levels within a design where various elements can be placed. Layers allow for easier editing of individual elements without affecting others.

12.Opacity

The degree to which something is transparent or opaque. Lower opacity makes elements semi-transparent, while 100% opacity makes them solid.

13.Pantone (PMS)

A standardized color matching system used in printing to ensure consistency across different materials and printers.

14.Pixel

The smallest unit of a digital image or display. Pixels are the tiny dots that form a screen image. Resolution is often measured in pixels.

15.RGB (Red, Green, Blue)

A color model used for digital screens, where colors are created by combining varying intensities of red, green, and blue light.

16.Resolution

The clarity of an image, often measured in dots per inch (DPI) for print or pixels per inch (PPI) for screens. Higher resolution images have more detail.

17.Saturation

The intensity or purity of a color. High saturation means the color is vivid and strong, while low saturation means it's more muted or washed out.

18.SVG (Scalable Vector Graphics)

A vector image format that allows graphics to be scaled to any size without losing quality. It's commonly used for web and print designs.

19.Vector Graphics

Graphics made up of lines, curves, and shapes, rather than pixels. Vector images can be resized without losing quality, making them ideal for logos and illustrations.

20. White Space (Negative Space)

The empty space around and between elements in a design. White space helps to improve readability, balance, and the overall aesthetic of a design.

21. Typeface

A set of characters of the same design, including letters, numbers, and symbols. Common typefaces include Arial, Times New Roman, and Helvetica.

22. Mockup

A visual representation of a design in its final form, often used to showcase how the design will look on a real product or platform.

23. Pantone Matching System (PMS)

A standardized color reproduction system used in the printing industry to ensure colors remain consistent across various printers and materials.

24. Favicon

A small icon that appears in the browser tab next to the page title, typically associated with a website.

25. Gradient

A gradual transition between two or more colors. Gradients are often used in backgrounds or to add depth and dimension to designs.

26. Content Management System (CMS)

A software application used for creating, managing, and modifying digital content, commonly used for web design. Examples include WordPress and Joomla.

27. Responsive Design

A design approach where the layout of a website or digital product adjusts to the size of the screen it's being viewed on, providing a seamless user experience across devices.

28. Flat Design

A minimalist design style that uses simple, two-dimensional elements without gradients or textures. It focuses on clean lines, bold colors, and straightforward typography.

29. Branding

The process of creating a unique identity for a company or product. This includes logos, typography, colors, and overall design, which convey the brand's values and message.

30.UI/UX Design

UI (User Interface) design focuses on the layout and interactive elements of a website or app, while UX (User Experience) design focuses on the overall experience and ease of use for the user.

31.Wireframe

A basic visual guide used in the planning phase of a web or mobile design. It outlines the structure, navigation, and content placement without focusing on details like colors or typography.

32.Typography Hierarchy

The arrangement of text in a way that emphasizes certain elements (such as headings, subheadings, and body text) to make the content easy to read and understand.

33.Raster Graphics

Images composed of a grid of individual pixels, often used for digital photos. Examples include JPEGs, GIFs, and PNGs.

34.Call to Action (CTA)

A prompt or instruction that encourages the user to take a specific action, such as "Click here" or "Buy now."

35.Monospaced Font

A type of font where every character occupies the same amount of horizontal space. Often used in coding and design that requires precise alignment.

36.Negative Space

The area around and between elements of a design, often used to create shapes or balance. It can be used creatively to add meaning or visual interest.

37.Vector File

A type of graphic file that uses vector graphics (lines, shapes) rather than pixels, making it infinitely scalable without losing quality.

38.Mockup

A prototype of a design that showcases how it will appear in its real-world application. This can include items like website layouts, packaging, and product designs.

39.Drop Shadow

A visual effect applied to text or images to create the illusion of depth by adding a shadow behind the object.

40.Wireframe

A visual guide to show the layout of a page, often used in the early stages of website and app design to map out structure and content flow.

41.UI Elements

Individual components that make up the user interface, such as buttons, sliders, checkboxes, and navigation menus.

42.Brand Guidelines

A set of rules that define how a company's branding elements (logos, typography, color schemes, etc.) should be used to maintain consistency across all marketing materials.

43.Color Palette

A selection of colors used consistently throughout a design. It's important for establishing visual harmony and reinforcing brand identity.

44.Design Brief

A document provided by a client that outlines the project's goals, expectations, target audience, and deliverables.

45.Mockup

A full-scale, detailed representation of how the final product will look. Often used to present designs to clients for feedback before final production.

46.Legibility

The ease with which text can be read, especially at smaller sizes. Choosing the right fonts, spacing, and contrast can improve legibility.

47.Vector Art

Art created with vector graphics that can be resized infinitely without loss of quality. It's commonly used for logos, icons, and illustrations.

48.Bleed Area

The part of a design that extends beyond the trim edge of the page to ensure there are no unintentional white borders after trimming.

49.Interactive Design

A design approach that focuses on the way users interact with digital products like websites and apps. It involves user-centered design principles.

50.Consistency

Maintaining uniformity across all design elements, ensuring that fonts, colors, spacing, and other elements are cohesive to create a unified visual experience.

Design Resources and Networking for New Creators

1. Behance

   •URL: www.behance.net

   •Description: Behance is one of the largest platforms for designers, where they can create portfolios, share their work, and find inspiration. It's a great place to receive feedback from other designers and grow your skills.

2. Dribbble

   •URL: www.dribbble.com

   •Description: Dribbble is a social network for designers where they can share their work-in-progress, design samples, and receive feedback. It's an excellent place for beginners to find their niche and learn from others.

3. Reddit (r/Design)

   •URL: www.reddit.com/r/design

   •Description: Reddit has many helpful subreddits for designers, such as r/Design, r/graphic_design, and others, where you can find advice, share your work, ask questions, and discuss the latest trends.

4. Instagram

   •URL: www.instagram.com

   •Description: Instagram has become a platform where many designers share their work, inspiration, and behind-the-scenes processes. Search for designers through hashtags like #graphicdesign, #logodesign, #branding.

5. Facebook Groups

   •URL: www.facebook.com/groups

   •Description: Facebook has many groups for designers, where you can share your work, ask questions, get advice, and support from fellow designers. For example, groups like "Graphic Design Inspiration" or "Designers Helping Designers" provide a wealth of useful information.

6. LinkedIn

   •URL: www.linkedin.com

•Description: LinkedIn is a professional social network where you can find connections with other designers, exchange experiences, and share your work. You can also join specialized groups focused on design.

7. Designspiration

•URL: www.designspiration.net

•Description: This is a platform for searching and saving design inspirations, where you can find design ideas, branding concepts, logos, fonts, and much more. It's great for building your portfolio or finding ideas for your projects.

8. Canva Design Community

•URL: www.canva.com

•Description: Canva is a popular tool for beginner designers. Their community actively shares tips, templates, and ideas, which helps beginners improve their design skills.

9. Designer Hangout

•URL: www.designerhangout.co

•Description: Designer Hangout is a community for designers offering chats, consultations, and support for designers at all levels. It's a great place to receive real-time feedback and learn from others.

10. YouTube (Design Channels)

•URL: www.youtube.com

•Description: YouTube is a massive platform for tutorials and guides on design. Look for channels that specialize in graphic design for beginners. Recommended channels include The Futur, Yes I'm a Designer, Will Paterson.

11. Adobe Live

•URL: www.behance.net/live

•Description: Adobe Live is a platform for live streams where professional designers host sessions, share their workflows, give advice, and answer questions. It's a great place for learning from professionals in real-time.

12. The Design Tip (YouTube Channel)

•URL: The Design Tip YouTube

•Description: A YouTube channel offering helpful tips for beginner designers, from tutorials to explanations of basic design principles.

13. Awwwards

•URL: www.awwwards.com

•Description: Awwwards is a platform that awards the best websites for design and innovation. It's a great place to study current web design trends and find inspiration for your projects.

14. Toptal

•URL: www.toptal.com

•Description: Toptal is a platform for freelancers, where you can find top-tier designers. Though it's focused on experienced professionals, beginners can find valuable advice through blogs and articles on the site.

15. Pinterest

•URL: www.pinterest.com

•Description: Pinterest is a visual search engine and inspiration platform. You can find millions of design ideas, logos, brandings, fonts, and more. It's also great for organizing your creative ideas into boards.

16. Designmodo

•URL: www.designmodo.com

•Description: Designmodo is an online resource for designers that includes articles, tools, and resources for creating web designs, graphics, interfaces, and more.

17. Fontspring

•URL: www.fontspring.com

•Description: Fontspring is an online marketplace for fonts for designers. It's a resource where you can find unique and professional fonts for your projects.

18. 99designs

•URL: www.99designs.com

•Description: A platform where designers can participate in contests and find work. It's a great place for beginners to practice on real projects and build their portfolios.

19. Canva Design School

•URL: www.canva.com/learn

•Description: Canva has its own "Design School" offering tutorials for beginners. It covers design basics, how to use Canva tools, and much more.

20. Designer News

•URL: www.designernews.co

•Description: A community for designers where you can share news, articles, and discussions on relevant design topics. It's also a great place for idea exchange and inspiration.

Other Resources for Design Beginners:

•Adobe Creative Cloud Tutorials (for mastering Photoshop, Illustrator, etc.).

•Skillshare and Udemy – Online courses for beginners in design.

•Font Squirrel – Free font download platform.

•Unsplash and Pexels – Free high-quality image platforms for your design projects.